BIRTH
MARKS

Also by Lucy and Dennis Guernsey
> REAL LIFE MARRIAGE

By Dennis Guernsey
> THOROUGHLY MARRIED
> IF I'M SO FREE, HOW COME I FEEL BOXED IN?
> A NEW DESIGN FOR FAMILY MINISTRIES
> ON BEING FAMILY (with R. S. Anderson)
> THE FAMILY COVENANT
> SOMETIMES IT'S HARD TO LOVE GOD

BIRTH MARKS

DR. DENNIS & LUCY
GUERNSEY

WORD PUBLISHING
Dallas·London·Vancouver·Melbourne

BIRTHMARKS

Scripture quotations marked NASB are from the *New American Standard
Bible,* © 1960, 1962, 1963, 1968, 1971, 1972, 1973, 1975, 1977 by The
Lockman Foundation, and used by permission. Scripture quotations
marked NIV are from the Holy Bible, New International Version,
copyright © 1973, 1978, 1984 by the International Bible Society, and used
by permission of Zondervan Bible Publishers.

Library of Congress Cataloging-in-Publication Data

Guernsey, Dennis B.
    Birth marks : breaking free from the destructive imprints of your
family history / by Dennis and Lucy Guernsey.
        p.   cm.
    ISBN 0-8499-0904-X
    1. Pastoral counseling.   2. Family psychotherapy.   3. Family —
Religious life.   I. Guernsey, Lucy, 1940-   .   II. Title.
BV4012.2.G84   1991
253.5 — dc20
                                                            91-9352
                                                            CIP

Printed in the United States of America

1 2 3 4 9 AGF 9 8 7 6 5 4 3 2 1

*This book is dedicated to the young adults
at Fuller Theological Seminary and the
California Institute of Technology (Caltech),
who have shown us through their journeys
how to be transitional people*

Contents

1.

Ghosts of the Past

Adoniram Judson Bell.* The name looked and sounded official but not familiar. *It must be a new client,* Dennis** said to himself as he looked over his counseling schedule for the day and considered the maze of people facing him with their problems and situations.

* The names used in this book represent real people whose identities have been changed for the sake of confidentiality. Usually the stories are combinations of life stories, although they may sometimes be hypothetical. In all cases it is our intent not to refer to anyone specifically. We have attempted to mask the stories and illustrations except in those cases where we, ourselves, are the examples. In those instances we have told the stories as we both understand them and/or experienced them.
** In the writing of this book, as was our custom in *Real Life Marriage,* we have chosen to refer to ourselves with our first names rather than switch back and forth between *he, she,* etc. We recognize the cumbersomeness of the style at times. We ask the reader's patience.

Mr. Bell, whoever he was, represented a mystery. No address. No telephone number. Only the secretary's penciled notation, "Very hesitant to give any information over the phone. Needed to be reassured that his coming and his going would be anonymous." His name made him doubly interesting. Adoniram Judson had been one of the very first missionaries from the U.S. to Burma, sometime in the early 1800s. Dennis wondered what the connection would be.

A. J. (Mr. Bell's nickname since birth) arrived in Dennis's office dressed in a three-piece gray pin-striped suit, complemented by spit-polished shoes and a firm handshake. He measured the office suspiciously as he entered and took a seat without hesitation.

He looked calm and in control. Dennis expected a sales pitch. Instead, A. J.'s story poured out immediately, almost like an erupting volcano. No sooner was he asked why he had come than he launched into a painful litany of confusion and doubt. He talked for thirty minutes straight, stopping only to breathe. It was clearly evident that his wardrobe and confident demeanor were a cover-up for the hurt that filled his life from dawn to dusk. He was in trouble. Life was out of control.

A. J. was a missionary casualty recently forced to return home against his will. He had been voted off the field by his fellow missionaries.

"They said I had a contentious spirit" was the reason he reported, without any show of visible emotion. He had served on the mission field for more than ten years only to be reassigned by his missionary agency to a support position in the States upon his return. Now, even that new job was in question.

As he talked of his experience, his bitterness about what had transpired on the mission field filled the counseling room. His journey had not been an easy one. He began his story in the present and then, at Dennis's prodding, worked backwards into the past.

The event that had precipitated A. J.'s removal from the mission field had been an out-of-control, bitter tirade he had launched against his fellow missionaries six months before at their yearly field council. He said he couldn't remember the exact reason he had become enraged (it was a combination of things that had built up over the years), but he did remember stalking out of the room screaming and yelling profanities, hurling wooden folding chairs as he exited.

The next day, his boss handed him a letter of dismissal and a one-way air ticket home for him and his family. They had exactly two weeks to pull everything together, pack their belongings, and be gone. His boss said they had "had enough of A. J.'s immaturity and childish tantrums." They were through warning him. He had outlived his welcome. Whoever or whatever had "called" him to Africa was now being overridden by the collective will of his fellow missionaries.

His return to the States had been chaotic. Needless to say, his departure from the mission field had been disastrous. He had pleaded, begged, and demanded that he be allowed to stay — all for naught. The goodbyes at the airport in the African capital had been strained. His wife had been humiliated by their departure and blamed him for their plight. Their three children were similarly confused. The flight home had been sullen and painfully quiet.

Since their return, the family had been in constant turmoil, with fighting every night at the dinner table. No one was happy, least of all A. J. He had been told by his mission agency to take some time off and to seek therapy immediately. To top it all off, he had begun to experience migraine headaches, whose cause, according to his physician, was pronounced stress.

What do we say to the A. J.'s in our lives? What do we say and how do we react if the A. J. happens to be us? We can handle the matter as a spiritual one, which Dennis imagined it was, at least in part. Certainly, his behavior at the moment and evidently historically couldn't be classified as "Spirit-filled."

Ironically, A. J. had treated his problems over the years as spiritual in nature. Later, in therapy, he talked of the many times he had repented for his outbursts of anger and his inability to contain his rage. He believed that he was a carnal Christian and that if only he could get his act together spiritually, his problems with controlling his emotions would be behind him. His discouragement, again compounded over the years, was that his spiritual prescriptions hadn't worked.

SEARCHING FOR EXPLANATIONS

In some ways, A. J. is like many of us. There are pockets of problems tucked away in our daily lives, problems that surface at the most inopportune and inappropriate times. We make promises to ourselves, to those we love, and to God about what we intend to do about them. We promise not to display the behavior again, only, to our chagrin, to be faced with the presence of the situation and its subsequent embarrassment another time in another place. Our promises become empty even though at the time we mean them with all of our hearts. Eventually, our promises to ourselves and to everyone else wear very thin.

Or, perhaps A. J.'s problems are psychological in nature. It's more and more fashionable to think in those terms. But, what do we mean when we say the problems are "psychological" in nature? Do his problems stem from the way he is thinking, or from a behavioral pattern that has been deeply reinforced over the years? Perhaps the issue has more to do with early childhood experiences between A. J. and his mother (i.e., it may be more psychoanalytically oriented).

As a therapist for more than twenty-five years, Dennis saw all of the above-mentioned spiritual and psychological issues as being potential answers.

What proved to be most helpful in A. J.'s situation relates to the heart of this book. The insights A. J. needed in order to sort out his particular situation were generational in nature, having their roots in his family past as those roots interacted, often unconsciously, with the present. The title of this book, *Birthmarks*, suggests that these root causes have been unhealthy, a kind of blemish or generational imperfection on the branches of his family tree. The key question becomes, What do we mean by "generational"?

A SCRIPTURAL KEY

A passage both Dennis and Lucy have come to appreciate more and more is found in the Old Testament Book of Job.

> Please inquire of past generations,
> And consider the things searched out by their fathers.
> For we are only of yesterday and know nothing,
> Because our days on earth are as a shadow.

Will they not teach you and tell you,
And bring forth words from their minds?
   (Job 8:8-10, NASB)

The Book of Job is probably the oldest book in the Bible, written before any of the others. Yet, in the dialogue between two of the central characters of the story, Bildad and Job, we find an insight that is relevant today even though it was written thousands of years ago. *Our past generations can teach us about ourselves* if we but ask them to speak.

In our modern day, two issues or trends seem to be relevant.

The first is the tendency in our culture for us to believe that whatever is important in terms of today is a function of today. That is, we all tend to live in the here and now. We are *the "now" generation.*

Certainly that's true in terms of planning for the future. For example, savings rates for American families are at an all-time low. Similarly, long-term debt is at an all-time high. We — those of us who represent the majority of citizens in the U.S. at the beginning of the 1990s — are willing to mortgage the future in order to protect the quality of our lifestyle in the present. That's the message behind the increasing national debt we keep hearing and reading about on television and in the newspapers.

If we don't want to think about the future, we even more don't consider the past. What is gone is gone, obsolete. Ten years in the past — let alone thirty, fifty, or one hundred years — seems like a long time ago. World War II, the war fought by our fathers and grandfathers, seems like ancient history. Too much of life has gone on since then.

Our rejection of the past has led to an ignorance of the past. In the academic discipline we are most acquainted with — marriage and family therapy (Dennis's specialty) — generational issues have become more and more relevant.*

In particular, "family systems theory" has caught the eye of the profession. Family systems theory suggests that recurring patterns in the present life of a family, both functional and dysfunctional, can be understood best when couched in terms of the history of the family, that is, their generational past. For example, patterns of anxiety, addictions such as alcoholism and drug abuse, patterns of emotional disruptions, and the victimizing of one or more persons in a family by others in their generation are understood to be generational in origin.

USING THE KEY

A. J.'s experience illustrates the importance of our generational past.

A. J. was born in 1946, the eldest son of a young couple who had married eight years earlier. His mother and father had met in school where they were studying to be missionaries, specializing in missionary medicine. It was their intention to go to the mission field in Africa at the end of their schooling.

---

* For the reader who is interested in learning about generational issues in greater depth, we suggest the following important sources: Murray Bowen, *Family Therapy in Clinical Practice* (New York: Jason Aronson, 1978); Michael E. Kerr and Murray Bowen, *Family Evaluation* (New York: W. W. Norton and Co., 1988); Edwin H. Friedman, *Generation to Generation: Family Process in Church and Synagogue* (New York: The Guilford Press, 1985).

Unfortunately, World War II intervened and A. J.'s father was drafted into the military. In 1942 he became a medic in the infantry due to his prior medical training. The father personally experienced some of the fiercest fighting in the war, in North Africa and Italy, and was decorated for bravery.

Tragically, when the father returned to the States after the war he was an emotionally broken man. He was never again able to generate the enthusiasm he once felt for the mission field, to the severe disappointment of A. J.'s mother. And although the father returned to school after the war using the G.I. Bill to get his teaching credential, he consistently kept himself aloof from the family, usually complaining about his physical condition in the process.

It was during these years of marital turmoil that A. J. grew up. In the hospital room following his birth, his mother had named him Adoniram Judson and dedicated him to the Lord to be the missionary she had never been allowed to be. He was kept constantly aware of that fact as she rehearsed over and over again for her family the circumstances surrounding his birth.

Although three more children were born after A. J., he was clearly his mother's favorite and he worked hard at never disappointing her. He went to Sunday School all his life, entered the same school his father and mother had attended (although it was now a Christian liberal arts college), and dedicated himself to missionary service while a young teenager. That A. J. was supposed to be a missionary was a foregone conclusion.

However, there were a number of other factors in A. J.'s generational past that also had a bearing on his current situation.

His maternal grandmother, like her daughter, had been active in church when she married, twenty years before A. J.'s mother had married. Unfortunately, as a young teenager she had become pregnant and had married A. J.'s grandfather, whom she did not love, when she was seventeen years old. A disgrace to the family at the time, the pregnancy became a family secret until it came to the surface in A. J.'s therapy. No one, to A. J.'s knowledge, had spoken of it to the grandmother.

In addition to the tragedy of the premarital pregnancy, the grandfather became a heavy drinker and habitually abused both his wife and his children. The grandfather's abuse of his family had never been acknowledged and had become one of the family's secrets as well.

The Sunday evening church service at which A. J. had been commissioned as a missionary had been the proudest day in his mother's life. He brought to therapy a picture taken at the time of his commissioning service. His mother was standing at the center of the picture, alongside her missionary son, as if the rest of the participants, including A. J.'s wife, were marginal in importance.

A. J. and his wife had gone to Africa believing that God had called them to serve Him in reaching that continent for Christ. Soon after their arrival, A. J. began to have problems, most of which had to do with his fitting into the established patterns of the missionary community. When, in his opinion, things weren't working, he wanted to charge in and fix them right away rather than wait until his fellow missionaries were willing to change. He was notoriously impatient. Within the first year he gained the reputation of being an irritant.

The solution of the field superintendent was to assign A. J. and his wife to a remote station where they would interact with their fellow missionaries least often. It worked marginally well for the first two terms on the field. Then in the middle of the third term (each term was four years in length) A. J. agitated for another assignment with greater authority, as befitted his seniority. His boss had put him off several times when the outburst occurred that led to his leaving the field.

During the third or fourth session of therapy with Dennis, when A. J. paused in his reconstruction of his generational past, Dennis asked, "A. J., were you really called to be a missionary or were you responding to your mother's call?" The words hung in the air.

Even though the question is obvious in retrospect, it had never entered A. J.'s mind. Dennis followed up. "Can you remember a time, in high school or in college, when you ever thought of being something other than a missionary?"

His response was immediate. A. J. remembered loving his math classes in high school as well as his physics classes. His physics teacher, A. J.'s favorite, suggested that he consider science or engineering in college. His SAT scores during his senior year seemed to support this advice.

When A. J. brought his enthusiasm home to share with his mother, she was quick to point out his "call" as a fourteen-year-old and the injunction not to "quench the Spirit of God" with his worldly desires. From that point on, he laid aside his thoughts of being an engineer and focused on becoming a missionary.

After several more sessions, A. J. came to grasp several generational issues that he needed to face as he sorted out his future. He learned he was not born in a vacuum. His upbringing had left him with several noticeable behavioral and emotional "birthmarks."

First, he was able to see that, beginning with his grandmother, the women in his family had been unable to fulfill their calling for God because of the emotional state of their spouses. Their marriages had limited their options for ministry. By the time the baton of service passed to A. J. he had to carry it forward lest he disappoint two generations of frustrated minister/missionary women.

Second, both his grandmother and his mother had been disappointed with the men they married. A. J. carried the responsibility to make up for those disappointing relationships. Consequently he had become his mother's subtly spoiled son through whom she lived out her needs and fantasies.

Third, the abusive patterns that were on the surface in his grandmother's marriage, and under the surface in his mother's (as evidenced by his father's probable depression), were a full-blown reality in his life, as demonstrated by his inability to cope with authority and the frustrations of living and working with people who weren't especially impressed with his abilities, at least not as impressed as his mother had been.

Last of all, there seemed to be a generational pattern of demonstrating emotional dysfunction through physical symptoms. This was the case in his father's response to his wartime experiences, a pattern of responses that took him out of contact with his family and with his eldest son in particular.

A grandmother's illegitimate pregnancy and unhappy marriage with its pattern of emotional and physical abuse, a father's terrible and debilitating experience during war, a mother's frustrated career expectations and subsequent unhappiness in marriage, her smothering love of her son due, as well, to her frustration with her marriage, and A. J.'s seemingly submissive spirit to his mother and to God all layered themselves generationally inside A. J.'s psyche.

His behavior on the day he stormed out of the meeting with his fellow missionaries, consumed by rage and throwing chairs to the side as he left, can certainly be explained not only in terms of his immediate emotional immaturity but also in terms of a generational history that damned from the beginning any possibility of his success as a missionary.

Within the next six months A. J. decided that he needed to change careers. He decided his "call" to be a missionary was inaccurate. He took a job with an executive-search firm specializing in the recruitment of very sophisticated scientists and engineers for the aerospace industry. He became very good at it and made more money than he ever thought possible.

He also made peace with the women in his life, especially his mother, and set himself the task of having a marriage that was unlike that of both his parents and his grandparents. His wife welcomed the change.

Finally, he became the coach of his daughter's Little League softball team, throwing himself into each game with the same enthusiasm he had expended in his relational conflicts before. He decided he was going to place a priority on being a father unlike the example set for him by his father.

His past generations had spoken. He had listened and as a result had come to some very significant conclusions and decisions.

SUGGESTIONS FOR THE JOURNEY

To some degree we can all identify with A. J. and the dilemmas he faced. It's not uncommon for us to live out the expectations of others rather than to find our own way through life. That's our dilemma. What's the solution?

It's our intention in this book to encourage you, the reader, in two crucial undertakings as you probe deeper into your own dilemmas: to look not only within but also backwards into your generational past *as* you look within. Looking within is what the interface between Christianity and psychology is all about. Looking backwards, we realize, might be something new, something unusual, even sometimes threatening. Borrowing a phrase from the Book of Job, what do you need to know as you begin to "inquire from the past"?

To begin with, *recognize that the power of the past, though awesome, need not be fearsome.* When you begin to ask hard questions about your past that may cause family blemishes or disturbing events to be revealed, anxiety can be expected to rise to the surface. You will need to distinguish between facts and fears. Family secrets and family patterns of dysfunction usually are rooted in our family's fears or anxieties. When faced head-on, the fears often prove to have been greater than the facts. The principle is best summed up in the words of U.S. Supreme Court Justice Louis Brandeis, "Sunlight is the best of all disinfectants."

To whatever degree you are exposing long-established psychological birthmarks, the inertia of the past will seek to inhibit your pursuit of truth in the present. As is true in the environment, so it is in our generational past: toxicity, the source of pollution, is harder to clean up than it was to deposit in the first place. What sometimes makes it hardest of all is facing the reality of what was or what is polluting.

The next principle in our inquiry of our past is to *look for explanations rather than excuses.* Whatever happened before doesn't excuse you from your responsibilities in the present. Just because your "imperfection" has its origin in your past doesn't let you off the hook. For example, in A. J.'s case, he still had to make some difficult choices and take responsibility for his immaturity even after he better understood the reasons for his behavior.

Third, it is important to *recognize that the past only influences the present; it doesn't determine it.* However powerful the currents of the past seem to be, it's possible to do something about them. You are not caught in an inexorable, predetermined pattern of dysfunction. With God's help, and perhaps the help of others, you can do something about what it is that hurts or bothers you. The story of the present is never written in permanent ink.

Our last suggestion for this journey into your family past is to *look for positive as well as negative examples.* For instance, who were your progenitors of faith? How, when, and through whom did the Gospel enter your family? Who were the successes as well as the "failures"? Who were the strong people, the positive influences? In your search, look for health as well as hurt.

As it was written in the Book of Job, centuries ago, the past will both teach us and tell us. We need only to listen in order to learn.

2.

Transitional People

This is a book about becoming a transitional person.*

A transitional person is someone who decides that dysfunctional family patterns, destructive behaviors which are transmitted through the generations, will stop with him or her. Ultimately it describes the work of Jesus Christ, God's only Son, who on our behalf changed the course of history for the human race. He became *the* transitional person for us.

A transitional person is also one who makes a decision, or a series of decisions, which help remove dysfunctional imperfections

* The introduction and this book in general is an expansion of an earlier book by Dennis entitled *The Family Covenant: Loving and Forgiving in the Christian Home* (Chicago: David C. Cook Publishing Co., 1984).

from his or her family so that the future course of history for that family is forever altered. The process of being a transitional person may be described as follows: First, a transitional person typically recognizes the need to struggle with his or her own agenda as it is contrasted with the different agenda of his or her family. Second, he or she is often required to make sacrifices in his or her own personal life on behalf of the welfare of the family. And, finally, the process requires a kind of death, and dying is never easy. It is difficult and often painful.

Whether the dysfunctional family "scar" is pervasive (such as chronic addictive behavior—alcoholism, chemical dependency, etc., or psychosomatic illness—having its causes in the mind rather than in the body) or idiosyncratic (behavior that tends to deal with relational stress using "cutoffs"), the patterns of imperfection have their genesis in deeply held emotional and intellectual grooves. Once a groove has been formed it can soon become a rut. Once a rut is formed it can determine the course of human traffic across the generations.

These "human traffic patterns" can only be changed if there is a transitional path or road of some kind. The key word is *transitional*. At the heart of the word is the idea of change, of passing from one state, condition, or idea to another. The focus is upon the "passing from." In literature, the effective use of transitions aids the reader and helps him or her follow the writer's ideas and logic. In life, transitional people stand as if they were on a bridge between two markedly different patterns of behavior or systems of relationship.

For example, in the New Testament the Philippian jailer who asked the transitional question "What must I do to be saved?" was willing to do what it took to change. The transitional person asks the question "What must I do to change so that others in my life will be free to choose for themselves how they will be?" We invite you to consider whether you can be an agent of change, a transitional person.

CHANGING "WHO?"

A tendency we have noticed in most people is that of being conscious of how or what others need to do to change themselves rather than being conscious of how or what they need to change about themselves. This is the problem of what is caught in our own eye — a speck of dirt or a beam of lumber. The natural human behavior is to want to change others before we change ourselves.

In marked contrast, the transitional person operates on her / himself first. We like to describe this in the metaphor of focusing a single lens reflex (SLR) camera. As you look through the lens, you see in the center of the picture a spot or circle that needs to be brought into focus for the picture as a whole to be clear. In most cases whatever you place in the center of the picture is what you focus upon. The transitional person resists the temptation to focus upon others, and focuses the picture upon himself or herself even though others are in the picture.

Take, for example, the story of Marva. Marva came to see Dennis because she was depressed and anxious. Her marriage was in shambles, her finances were in chaos, and she was neither sleeping nor resting at night. She was agitated and anxious. As she began to relate her story, it was very clear that her focus was upon others in her life, especially her husband, rather than upon herself. According to Marva, her husband was refusing to put forward any effort to keep the company he had founded from going bankrupt. Consequently, she was desperately trying to run the business, pay the bills, and mother her two children. She was angry most of the time.

After listening, Dennis used the metaphor of the SLR camera to help Marva see that when she looked through the lens of her life she focused on her husband. In her view, if he would only change, then things would be OK.

As therapy continued, Dennis consistently asked Marva to listen to herself and ask the question "Whose image is in the center of the picture?" Over the weeks, she gradually came to focus upon herself rather than upon her husband. The more she focused upon herself as an agent of change, the more she felt empowered and the more her depression and anxiety lifted.

She was able to put the pieces of her past into perspective, especially that of her emotionally ill mother, and she was able to see herself as being in charge of her life. Her depression and anxiety related directly to her feeling that she was not in control of her own destiny. When that perception changed, she changed. She began the work of becoming a transitional person for her family.

In addition to changing herself, Marva realized that although she couldn't change her husband, she could change the way she related to him. In so doing, she changed the nature of their relationship. Relationships can be thought of as being like an algebraic equation. The factors on either side of the equal-sign are balanced. When one side of the equation changes, the other side of the equation is forced to change as well.

In Marva's case, her "self-surgery" changed two things: she stopped nagging her husband about the things she wanted done, and she began to write him notes and letters whenever she had something important to say to him. In the past, a verbal exchange quickly deteriorated into shouting and yelling with all the usual accompanying invective. When the nagging ceased, the communication moved from chaos to order. When the letters began, the emotional tone of their exchanges moved from anger to reason.

Finally, in terms of "who" it is that needs to change, Dennis challenged Marva to take prayer seriously and to ask God to become active in their lives. Soon she began to take responsibility upon herself to ask God to change her relationship with her husband. The equation changed on both sides of the equal-sign.

When Dennis last talked with Marva, she was working in a job not associated with her husband's company. She was feeling more secure about the future. And, she had given up responsibility for changing her husband. That was his and God's responsibility.

CHANGING "WHAT?"

The transitional person focuses upon generational patterns as they are manifested in three areas of family life.

The first area is *relational* patterns. In order to begin identifying your family's generational patterns, ask yourself the following questions: When people in my family get together, how would I describe the nature and quality of their behaviors toward one another? Do they gossip about others or about one another? Do they talk to one another through an intermediary rather than in direct conversation? In terms of their relationship, do they deal with feelings as well as with facts? Are they conscious of how they relate to one another as well as what they talk about? Is there a conscious keeping of secrets from one another, rather than a sense of trust and disclosure? Is the relationship a fundamentally balanced one or are the persons imbalanced in their relationship with each other? For instance, does someone dominate the conversation, thus forcing the other into the habitual role of listener, or is there a shared time of talking and listening?

Now, look back at the previous paragraph. You will see that there are several questions with two answers. Each of the questions has a relationally safe and balanced answer, and each has a relationally unsafe and unbalanced one. Those families who function mostly on the unsafe and unbalanced side tend to be families often plagued with problems of emotional distance, unresolved conflict, and relational abuse. That is, they tend to be more dysfunctional than other families. Those families whose answers fall on the more safe and balanced side tend to have emotional closeness, and experience greater conflict resolution and relational comfort.

Transitional people learn to keep in focus the camera lens through which they view family relationships. Rather than becoming caught up in the *content* of a conversation, they begin to listen to the *context* of the conversation. Most often the nature of a relationship is evidenced by how people communicate with one another rather than by what they are communicating about.

What needs to change in most families is the context of their relationships, their communicational patterns. Transitional persons begin by becoming observers of how those they love relate to one another. Then they begin the process of relating differently.

The second area that the transitional person focuses upon is his or her own *personal perceptions and ideas.* Rather than trying to change how others think, transitional people commit themselves to changing their own thinking.

An example from the New Testament comes to mind. With the coming of Christ and the call of the Apostles, Christianity in its earliest forms was mostly a Jewish sect. Not until after the day of Pentecost and Peter's sermon recorded in Acts 2 were the Gentiles even thought of as being eligible to become followers of Christ.

Then, in Acts 10 there is the marvelous story of the Apostle Peter's encounter with the Gentile Cornelius, a Roman army officer. In the story, Cornelius is instructed to find Peter in order to have his seeking after God rewarded. Simultaneously, in a dream, Peter hears a voice instructing him to put aside his parochial and provincial thinking. The same dream was repeated three times. When Peter awoke, Cornelius' servants found him and told him of their master's desire to know God. Peter then knew what his dream meant. Gentiles were to be equal partners in the Gospel with the Jews. The followers of Christ were no longer to be a Jewish elite but were to come from all parts of the world.

Later, at the Jerusalem Council when this issue was publicly debated (Acts 15), Peter's voice was heard on the side of those who would freely and fully embrace gentile converts to Christ.

In terms of the family of God and early church history, Peter's thinking radically changed us all. We are the beneficiaries of that change to this day. Peter qualifies as a transitional person.

The third area the transitional person focuses upon is *personal habits.* Those habits of how we do things, the routines and rituals of daily life, are often generational in origin but personal in expression.

We have a friend who, upon doing his family genogram (a tool we'll describe in the next chapter), discovered that in every previous generation on his father's side of the family, someone was an alcoholic. In some generations there were several, mostly males. In every case, this particular "birthmark" had a disastrous effect upon that generation.

Deciding that he would become a transitional person, at least for his own children, our friend concluded that he would from that day forward completely abstain from drinking alcohol. He had been only a casual drinker, with a beer here and a glass of wine there, but his decision was that the risk was too great for him to play the odds. At least for those who followed in his lineage, the cycle would be broken. He would make sure that his children had a choice.

Personal habits such as eating patterns, physical exercise routines, and the handling of anger fall into generational categories which have personal consequences. The transitional person begins with her / himself believing that the benefits of his / her decision may spread to those they love.

CHANGING "WHY?"

Why go to the effort of becoming a transitional person?

One reason is for your own personal happiness. It's not wrong to make decisions that will remove unhealthy generational imperfections and free you from dysfunctional tendencies if that decision is made in the context of relational responsibility, that is, in a way that looks after others' interests as well as your own (cf. Phil. 2:3 ff.).

Another reason to become a transitional person, and probably the most common one, is to relieve interpersonal pain. Nothing is more painful (or ugly) than to see those you love being hurt or hurting others. Whether this manifests itself in extreme sibling rivalry, through family members not talking to or seeing one another, or in other distressing ways, when you realize that somehow you are participating in the hurt you see going on, the pain often seems more than you can bear.

Suppose, for example, your son decides to marry at a very early age, say, eighteen. Suppose also, that the girl he decides to marry is someone you would never choose for him. In the depths of your heart you know that he has been "seduced, hogtied, and bamboozled" by this young woman.

Now, suppose two or three years go by and you now have a grandchild, a boy who will carry on the family name. One weekend you receive a telephone call from your twenty-one-year-old son asking if he can move in with you. He and his young wife are separating and considering divorce.

Next, as his parents, suppose you have recognized patterns about the way he has treated your daughter-in-law that resemble patterns you yourselves went through before he was born and that you saw lived out in your own parents' marriages years before. You married when you were eighteen and twenty as did your parents before you.

What do you say to him? How do you broach the subject? You don't like his wife and probably think that for him to be out of the marriage would be best. But, you've never liked the thought of divorce and even have some serious theological questions about it. What will happen to your grandson? His mother will likely get custody under today's laws. Will you ever see him again?

One of Dennis's clients found herself in this kind of situation. Her eldest son, the apple of her eye, surprised her one day with the news that he was getting married at age eighteen to someone the mother had never met. The subsequent marriage ended in divorce. And, her displeasure with the relationship had played a definite factor in the unhappiness between the marriage partners.

During their discussion about the issues involved, Dennis's client realized that she had been part of the problem rather than part of the solution. She had wanted so much for her son that she had not been subtle in communicating her displeasure. As she allowed herself to reflect on the preceding two years, hundreds of incidents of hurt came to mind. She was faced with a dilemma. What would she do?

She decided that she would "repent" (she used that word to describe her decision) and be reconciled to her daughter-in-law whether or not her son decided to remain married to her. Dennis remembers her reflections on her own earliest married years and the strain between her and her mother-in-law. Unconsciously she had replicated the pattern, and her son's marriage had suffered.

Dennis's client sought out her daughter-in-law, and they were able to work through some, if not all, of their problems. They were reconciled even though the marriage didn't survive. The primary beneficiary of the reconciliation was the grandson. His mother and his grandmother were able to become friends even though his parents weren't. The mother-in-law and the daughter-in-law remained in contact with one another, and the relationship prospered to the point that the grandmother was invited to her daughter-in-law's wedding two years later. Dennis's client had responded to the interpersonal pain she was experiencing and, as a result, she became a role model for reconciliation. She had removed the "birthmark" of estrangement and had become a transitional person—at least as far as her grandson was concerned.

CHANGING "HOW?"

In becoming a transitional person, it is an absolute necessity to *take ownership of whatever it is you recognize needs to change.* Taking ownership doesn't mean taking responsibility for everything. It's too easy for some people to hold themselves responsible for anything and everything that is wrong. People who chronically take responsibility for everything are as unrealistic about their role as those who chronically take responsibility for nothing. No one is "always" at fault. No one is "always" wrong. No one is "always" right.

By ownership we mean taking hold of your own life and allowing others to take hold of their own lives. For some, this involves holding on tighter. For others, it means letting go. The paradox of ownership is that you cannot fully name Jesus Christ as Lord unless you have taken ownership and responsibility for yourself. Until you do, you have nothing to yield. You can only yield what you yourself control.

Also of great importance in the matter of "how" we change is the presence of others who will be with us in the process. While there is something very lonely about becoming a transitional person, the support of others is tremendously helpful, even vital.

The journey is best traveled with others rather than alone. Therefore, we suggest you find others who will become fellow travelers on the path. Together, you can become a formidable force for good. Traveling alone is unnecessarily more difficult. Traveling with others is surprisingly empowering, as "Much Afraid" discovered in *Hind's Feet on High Places* by Hannah Hurnard.

Last of all, in terms of "how" we change, is the need to recognize *the importance of the grace of God in the process.* Grace is God's support for us given to accomplish what we cannot do for ourselves.

Two thoughts about grace:

First, Jesus Christ knows what it is to need grace. On the day he was crucified he stumbled from his trials and beatings, the sheer weight of the cross he was carrying causing him to fall. A man named Simon of Cyrene was forced by Roman soldiers to follow Jesus and carry the cross upon which he would be crucified. When Simon's knees buckled from the heaviness of his ordeal, he knew what it meant to be a transitional person with more weight than he could bear. At that moment there was nothing romantic and glorious about what he was experiencing.

So it is with transitional people. When they are faced with the choices they must make that will change the direction of their lives and the lives of their families, they find the experience is often arduous and demanding. They cannot be blamed for wanting to run from it. It is reasonable to whisper an inaudible prayer, "Nevertheless, not my will but thy will be done," as Christ prayed in the Garden of Gethsemane.

Second, the assistance afforded Christ at the

moment of his greatest trial came in the form of a human shoulder offered by someone who came alongside and gave aid. We draw attention to this fact because of the very human tendency in all of us to believe that we must "do it ourselves." We feel that to need help is to be weak, that to be strong is to reject help: that's our human fallacy, which is exactly the point. God's grace is for the times of our weakness and not just for the times of our strength. The norm is for God's grace to come to us wrapped in human form—the arm that holds us when we are overcome with grief, the voice that speaks encouragement to us when we want to quit, the person who listens to us when, in our trials, we are overwhelmed. When it comes to the presence of grace in the life of a transitional person, God is unusually incarnational, that is, God's love for us is made known to us through a human person's presence and actions.

CHANGING "WHEN?"

The last issue for discussion on becoming a transitional person is timing. How do you know when you are ready to begin? You are ready when you believe that you understand the complexity of your family's "birthmarks," when you are prepared for resistance from others, and when you accept the fact of the momentum of generational patterns and believe you will have the endurance to overcome discouragement. If your response is to feel overwhelmed by the challenge, then good. As Jesus said, you must count the costs before you start.

We point out first the problem of *complexity*. It's rarely simple to carry out a desire to change. You will soon find that the problems faced by a transitional person are intricately tangled, with more loose ends than tight knots. There will be more uncertainty than certainty, more doubt than faith. It is for times like these that we need the grace of God and the presence of fellow travelers. You must be aware of at least a semblance of what you face before you can think about beginning.

Second is the problem of *resistance*. We want to believe that those we love will choose health over illness, pleasure over pain, relationship over alienation, beauty over ugliness. Such is often not the case. You should expect more resistance than cooperation. Disappointment is the norm rather than success, especially at the beginning. People don't like to change, and the presence of a transitional person in their midst threatens them with just that demand. The human mobile of life will move when you move, but the people in the mobile may not like the movement. You must be patient.

And finally, there is the problem of *momentum*. Generational patterns and their consequences behave much like a super tanker in the water. The captain may see a problem and give the order to change direction, but the weight of such a large vessel will carry it through the water for miles before the captain's command is fulfilled. The more deeply entrenched is the imperfect pattern and the more generations it has been operable in a family, the greater the momentum, and the harder it is to stop the process. Generational dysfunctional scars are the toughest of all imperfections to remove, so again, be patient and don't be overcome with discouragement.

Our hope is that the journey we will take together through this book will be part of God's grace and strength for you. We encourage you to come along with us and to become a transitional person.

3.

The Trek Upstream

A friend of ours, known to be a wise and savvy businessman, is a successful builder who has developed several significant projects in Southern California. Because of his reputation as a developer of projects similar to the one under consideration by a local city government, he was invited to submit a bid for the redevelopment of a large piece of property that had been overcome with urban blight. He, as well as other developers, submitted his bid, and fortunately, he thought, his was chosen.

He moved quickly, creating plans for how the site would be developed, always keeping in mind the difficulties typically associated with such a project. To his amazement, the plans as a whole sailed through the approval process, and he moved to find financing. He was amazed at what appeared to be the simplicity of the deal.

Because of the size of the construction loan (more than $5,000,000), his out-of-state lender required him to submit a geologic study even though the redevelopment agency and the city's master planners had waived the requirement. The lender was being cautious because of his institution's suspicion of California projects (i.e., the relatively high incidence of earthquakes) as well as the requirements of its own regulatory agencies. When the geologist's preliminary report was handed in, the bomb dropped.

Buried six feet beneath the surface of the ground in the middle of the parcel was an old oil storage tank that had deteriorated badly. When the geologist looked back into the history of the property he discovered that the city had previously built and subsequently bulldozed a fire station on the site. At the time of its demolition, the fact and presence of the fuel storage tank were ignored. The contractor simply covered the hole, smoothed the dirt, and collected his money.

In the ensuing years the oil storage tank had rotted and had discharged its contents into the soil for hundreds of feet outward and downward. The cost for cleaning up the mess would run into the hundreds of thousands of dollars. The amount equaled the developer's profit margin for the whole project.

Even though the city's attorney advised the city council that the responsibility ultimately was the city's, the council voted to pass the costs for the clean-up on to the redevelopment agency, who in turn told the developer that they would pass most of the costs on to him. Under normal circumstances, the process of passing the buck would slowly have continued until the issue of who would pay for the clean-up was settled. Then, the development would have gone forward.

Unfortunately, the lender, who had asked for the geologic report in the first place, backed out of the deal, citing the developer's failure to perform according to a predetermined time schedule (which not surprisingly equaled the amount of time it took to determine the extent of the damage from the sunken tank). With his funding gone, our friend had to go back to ground zero, only to find that interest rates had risen significantly in the meantime and the project would cost him thousands of dollars more if the loan had to be funded by another institution.

At the time of our conversation, our friend was ready to throw in the towel and walk away from the whole mess, losing thousands of dollars and months of work as a result of the situation. His only recourse was a lawsuit against the city and the redevelopment agency. He dreaded his options.

What lay beneath the ground, buried years before as a result of someone else's negligence, had risen to the surface and had effectively sabotaged his project. He was out a lot of time and money and had experienced a great deal of frustration. Bitter and weary of the situation, he was finding it hard to be philosophical about it.

THE TOXICITY OF THE PAST

That sunken oil tank is like the toxic issues of our family histories that have been buried for scores of years. The issues, whatever they are now, seemed innocuous at the time. Probably no one had really taken them seriously. Or, if the seriousness was recognized, the problems were covered with the soils of denial and dishonesty, surfacing in a subsequent generation as a relational deformity, a behavioral mutation that defies explanation.

All families have an "oil spill" of one sort or another in their history. It's not the presence of the pollution that is the ultimate problem. How we handle the problem when we know it's there is far more important.

What can we know about our "birthmarks" by looking into our generational past and what can be done about them? These are the two major questions we need to ask ourselves. What we need are tools to do the generational "dig" much as the geologist had to dig as a part of his environmental impact study for the lending institution.

The "tool" we would like to give you as you begin your process of generational discovery is called a genogram.

BUILDING A GENOGRAM

A genogram resembles a family tree (i.e., a genealogy) with at least two significant additions: it contains not only the information about who lived when, but also what the quality of those individuals' relationships was and what, if any, were the significant events that marked their lives. The idea of a genogram is to gather in one place, in the form of a diagram, the relational history of a family. From that relational history we are able to question ourselves and to learn what it is we need to know in order to better understand ourselves.*

* For a full description of the creation of a genogram, see Monica McGoldrick and Randy Gerson, *Genograms in Family Assessment* (New York: W. W. Norton, 1985). The symbols for the genogram were standardized by the Task Force of the North American Primary Care Research Group chaired by Monica McGoldrick. They are part of the public domain.

Creating your own genogram involves three steps: (1) diagramming your family patterns or family tree, (2) sketching your family relationships, and (3) recording pertinent family information and significant events.

Diagramming Family Patterns

The genogram involves the use of a set of symbols depicting gender, birth order, marital relationships, and other necessary information such as adoption, abortions, etc.

Each family member is represented by a box for a male or a circle for a female:

The symbols are connected by a line indicating the biological or marital relationship between individuals. A marital relationship is indicated as follows:

—a separation is indicated by a single slash through the marital relationship line,

—and a divorce is indicated by a marital line with two slashes.

Where there have been multiple marriages and divorces, the relationships are depicted in chronological order moving from left to right.

If a couple is living together and/or the two are unmarried the relationship is indicated with dotted lines.

A death is indicated with an X inside the box or circle with the date of the death recorded alongside.

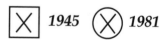

Children are indicated by their appropriate gender symbols with the eldest child appearing farthest left on the marital line and the youngest on the far right.

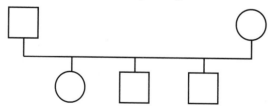

Twins are depicted as follows:

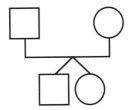

Adopted or foster children are indicated by a dotted line connected to the parent's marital line in the same way a solid line is used to show a child's blood relationship to his or her parent.

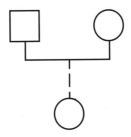

Sketching Family Relationships

What makes a genogram different from what we know to be a "family tree" is the insertion of symbols designed to indicate the level or quality of relationship existing between the various family members.

The most common way to indicate the quality of the relationships is to use one of the following six symbols:

—Overly close or enmeshed: ≡≡≡≡≡≡

This symbol indicates a relationship in which the participants are so involved or identified with one another that their feelings and thinking are fused. When you think of one person you almost always automatically think of the other. Sometimes their fusion is a kind of smothering or overprotective relationship. Or, instead, the relationship may be one of extreme dominance and submission. Whatever the relationship, it is hard to separate one from the other.

—Overly close and conflicted:

This symbol indicates a relationship that is both fused and very conflicted and angry. Often it is a relationship in which the two participants, though overly identified with one another, are unable to live peacefully together. Such a relationship would be characterized by the ambivalence of the simultaneous existence of both love and hate.

—Conflicted:

Chronic conflict between family members is indicated by a single jagged line. Usually this symbol is reserved for relationships in which conflict is habitual, demonstrating little, if any, closeness. These are the people who seem to have made fighting and conflict into an art form.

—Loving or close:

These relationships, which are for the most part healthy, indicating a strong but not binding closeness, are shown by two parallel lines. How the closeness is demonstrated is secondary to the accepted fact that the closeness exists. The participants "feel" the love and closeness between them.

— Distant: ● ● ● ● ● ● ● ● ● ● ● ● ●

This type of relationship, in contrast with a close or loving one, would probably involve a biological or legal relationship such as that between a parent and a child whose behaviors fail to typify caring or nurturing between the two.

— Estranged or cut-off:

This final symbol, signifying the emotional cut-off, is quite common. It represents a relationship between two people who are no longer communicating and whose relationship has been effectively severed. Usually, some event or confrontation marked the beginning of the cut-off.

Recording Pertinent Family Information

This is the phase of the genogram that involves gathering the family story. What were the events that function as markers in the history of the family? The interpretive section about A. J.'s life found at the end of chapter 1 is an example of what we're talking about.

When were people born and what were the circumstances surrounding their birth? When and why did people stop talking to one another? When were the migrations, the changes of homes and houses? Why did people move? Who went and who stayed? When did people die? How did they die?

Did they have any hurtful patterns such as addictions, family abuse, recurring illnesses? What were the circumstances in which they lived, their culture, their religious beliefs and values, their educational levels, etc.?

The more data you gather, the more clearly the mirror of your past will reveal your "birthmark" patterns. As you get involved with the process, more questions regarding this phase of the genogram will occur to you. Write your questions down and find an answer for them if at all possible.

Write the data down on a separate piece of paper and use it when you refer to the genogram itself.

Just about now, you are probably asking yourself if it's worth the work, effort, and possible pain to push forward and work on your own genogram. We don't blame you. We've asked ourselves the same question.

What follows is the story of one of Dennis's students concerning the process she went through in the discovery and initial clean-up of the "pollution" in her generational past.

DELLA'S STORY

Della began by telling Dennis of her experience in the middle of the previous work day. She'd been sitting in front of her computer screen for more than three hours and had accomplished nothing. She couldn't keep her mind on business. It kept wandering from her financial analysis of a client's proposal to the project she was completing for her after-hours seminary course on pastoral counseling.

She had chosen, as her term project, the research and creation of her own genogram. What had begun as a lark had become an obsession. She couldn't stop thinking about it. Why? Was it because she was beginning to understand some of her own deeply held longings and feelings? The answer just couldn't be that simple. Or, maybe it was.

Della had graduated from a college in western Washington seven years earlier and had settled into a comfortable job in the Seattle area. Because she was bright, personable, and willing to work long hours, her career had flourished. She was in her late twenties and single. Her friends from college were either married or panicked because they weren't. She felt oddly out of step. She was neither married nor panicked, but still she was restless.

The key to her restlessness had been the genogram. When she first approached the task, she was terrified. What if she found deformities on the "face" of her family that would blow it apart? Maybe she hadn't had the happy childhood she thought she'd had. Her class in abnormal psychology in college had worried her at the time. Fortunately, she thought, the semester ended before she probed too deeply. She was more interested in beginning her own career than in walking around in the "muck and goo" of her family's imperfections.

Something was different this time. She didn't know what.

Another key to her restlessness seemed to be her growing interest in serving in the church. She was the first Christian she knew of in her family.

She loved the involvement. She had been asked to serve as a deaconess (the first single woman in her church ever to have been asked), and she was thrilled.

Everyone else seemed to abhor the politics of the parish council but she loved it. Her interest in congregational life had provoked her to enroll in her first seminary course. In fact, her friends in the young singles group began referring to her as "Rev." She laughed with them while, inside, she liked the thought of studying the Bible. There seemed to be so much that she didn't know.

Copies of the questionnaire* she had developed for the genogram had been sent to all her living relatives and had generated an incredible amount of information, even though several had not been returned. Sure, there were family secrets, but she could already tell that her fears about the family's neuroses had for the most part been exaggerated.

What excited her was the questionnaire that had been returned in the previous day's mail. No one in her family even knew her great-step-aunt on her mother's side was still alive. Yet, there she was, ninety-three years old, a spinster, living in a retirement home in upstate New York. Her completed questionnaire was a window into Della's maternal grandfather's past.

Three generations before, in the early 1920s, Della's grandfather on her mother's side had migrated from the East Coast to the state of Washington. She learned from her other sources of information that there had been a severing of relationships, and her grandfather had solved his own personal dilemma by moving west. He never looked back, and he refused to have anything to do with his family "back east." He said only that he was an "orphan" and didn't want to talk about it. His

---

* A sample questionnaire has been included in the appendix. Edit it as you see fit and make it your own. Our thanks to Karen Klemetson, Angie Martin, and Kathie Stratmeyer for the use of their questionnaires as examples.

new wife went along with the cut-off, and he excitedly plugged into her family and made it his own as well as hers. The East Coast vanished.

Della's research uncovered the source of her grandfather's cut-off. According to her newly found great-step-aunt, her grandfather had been the only child of her wealthy great-grandfather's second wife. Their marriage had been a December/June affair. The great-grandfather's grown children had been scandalized. He had married the household maid, a much younger woman, whom the grown children of his first wife believed was only after his money. Della's great-grandfather had died when his son was very young, and two years later the great-grandmother had died as well, leaving Della's grandfather an orphan. Neither had left a will. Tragically, the child's grown half-brothers and sisters refused to take him in and instead chose to endow his care in a local orphanage.

Della's grandfather left the orphanage when he was sixteen and migrated west. It was there that he began a new life, putting the pain of the past behind him.

Although Della suspected something like this in her grandfather's past, what particularly interested her was the additional information from her genogram source.

On paper, she learned for the first time of her half-aunt, three generations before, who had been an aide to one of the earliest woman's suffrage leaders, Anna Howard Shaw.

Shaw, a Boston University–trained physician and Methodist minister, had recruited the aunt, a Methodist minister herself, to the newly emerging woman's movement. Together, in the late 1880s, they along with Susan B. Anthony had founded the National Woman's

Suffrage Association. Della's aunt, always in the background deferring to the more powerful Shaw, was a part of the passing of the 19th Amendment to the Constitution giving women the right to vote.

There it was, in black and white, at least a partial explanation for Della's restlessness — the twin strains of social activism and ministry wrapped up in her relative, one woman living in the late 1800s, generations before. No one else in Della's family shared even a whit of interest in the things of God. Only Della. That is, until now.

As she read the letter attached to the genogram questionnaire it was as if she could reach back and touch her ancestor's psyche. Della's social conscience always had been greater than that of her peers. She had found her soul-mate. Maybe, just maybe, Della's calling was to the ministry, to the intersection of the church's life with the world, just as had happened for her progenitor years before. At least now Della understood her own longings better and could tie her feelings to something other than her subjective present.

Though Della's story had begun years before, her task now was to add her chapter to the story and be consistent with herself. Her seminary work took on new meaning. Perhaps it presaged a new direction. Now she understood why it was important that she be open to God's call to do something different with her life.

As they discussed the implications of Della's genogram, Dennis reassured her that all families have an "oil spill" of one sort or another in their history. What had begun as a classroom project became a life-changing discovery. Della's story is an example of the good and the positive growth that can come out of the process of building a genogram.

SOME WORDS OF CAUTION

For many, the creation of a genogram is often an anxiety-provoking experience. Our past is sometimes filled with stories with which we are not prepared to deal. What we suggest, as a precaution, is to work on your genogram with a group of fellow travelers who are working on theirs at the same time. When sensitive issues come up in your family history, talk about them in the group. If you begin to feel overwhelmed, find someone wise whom you can trust and with whom you can talk through your fears and anxieties. A pastor or a therapist is often trained to give help and support in this kind of dialog.

Next, be patient. Some in your family may take issue with the questions you are asking. It's not uncommon for relatives to become incensed at the thought of the past being "dredged up." Rather than push, look for your family's "snitch." Every family has someone who has kept track of the family secrets. Usually they're not malicious with the information; they're just interested. Talk to them even if you have to phone them long distance to do so. Interview as many people in person as you can. Use the genogram as an opportunity to build and strengthen your relationships with your family. The time will be well spent.

Finally, if you run into a blank wall, accept the fact that you've gone as far as you can go and let the issue drop. You can only do what you can do.

In the next few chapters we will try to give you the tools to understand what you've found out. We'll try to interpret your genogram with you.

4.

A Case Study of Generational Anxiety

Della's story in the previous chapter gives us a good look at someone who was able to gain from the construction of a genogram. The most dramatic benefit Della experienced was the reduction of generational uneasiness that pervaded her family on her mother's side. Before she began her genogram, she couldn't put her finger on the reason for that uneasiness, but it was true that too many questions were unanswered. It was as if a historical vacuum had existed ever since the time her grandfather moved to the Pacific Northwest.

As she led her family through several discussions about their past, her research into her family history acted as a catalyst for them. Initially, her grandfather resisted strongly, but eventually even he went along with the collective wishes and curiosity of his family. What began as an assignment ended as a life-changing event, especially for Della.

The generational uneasiness experienced by Della and her family goes under another name in the family therapy literature. It's called "chronic generational anxiety." In the hundreds of genograms we've evaluated, including our own, the most powerful use of the genogram is its value in helping people uncover the sources of this anxiety in whatever forms it takes.

In dealing with chronic generational anxiety in families, two other issues lie beneath the surface. These issues have to do with the relative hurtfulness of this anxiety to families and with whether or not a relationship with God protects us from such hurtfulness. Most of us would hope that it does. We want to believe that a relationship with God will correct whatever unsightly "birthmarks" there are, if any, that lie undiscovered somewhere in our generational past.

Evidence suggests otherwise. Too many fine, dedicated men and women of God find themselves dealing with issues that seem to extend beyond the boundaries of their immediate family. When we press deeper into the family stories, more often than not, an explanation for the uneasiness, or problem, becomes visible and tangible.

As evidence for our view that a relationship with God doesn't insulate us from the effects of our generational past, we lay before you the following genogram from the Old Testament, a three-generational family story which begins with Abraham and Sarah and ends with Jacob and Rachel.

Everyone agrees on the importance of these heroes and heroines. Abraham and Sarah are held up as key examples of faith in the New Testament Book of Hebrews (chap. 11), and Abraham is described by the Apostle Paul as "the father of the faithful" (Rom. 4:1 ff.). What can we learn from them about ourselves as we evaluate their life stories and the effects of their decisions upon their own generations?

BROTHERS WHO HATE

Suppose, for purposes of illustration, we were trying to explain the alienation between Jacob and Esau as recorded in chapters 32 and 33 of Genesis. The passage states that Jacob was "greatly afraid and distressed" as he anticipated his encounter with his brother Esau after several years of having been separated from him (Gen. 32:6). Jacob was upset and highly anxious.

If Jacob were alive today, let's imagine that it's just possible you could be the person he might seek out for counsel as he contemplated his impending and probable confrontation with Esau. Given the previous history of anger and rancor, involving cheating and trickery by Jacob's mother, Rebekah, and Jacob, his anxiety is understandable (see Genesis 27). Suppose, again, you took the time with Jacob to work through his genogram with him. What might you discover, and what might you say to him?

Remember, the purpose of a genogram is to provide insight into the relational and behavioral patterns of the present in terms of the generational past. What is happening now can most often be explained by what has happened before.

Here, then, on page 56, is a fully diagrammed three-generational genogram for Jacob and Esau, stretching all the way back to Abraham and Sarah.

What is of importance are the recurring patterns within and between the generations, in Jacob's and Esau's family beginning as far back as the relationship between Abraham and Sarah.

OVERLY CLOSE BOUNDARIES

When you look at the genogram, you'll notice that each generation has a set of relational lines between a parent and a child that indicates an overly close parent-child relationship. Isaac received a "double portion" from Abraham and Sarah, probably because of the circumstances surrounding his miraculous birth. In the next generation, Isaac had his favorite child, Esau, and Rebekah had her favorite as well, Jacob. What we see in this account is how the overcloseness causes the parents constantly to play favorites, thus allowing the children to manipulate their parents against one another, leading to serious sibling rivalry.

Although it's not recorded on this genogram, the pattern of overcloseness continued in the generation of Isaac's son Joseph. In his own generation, Joseph, like his father, Jacob, also paid a price in a traumatic way. He was abandoned by his brothers because of their jealousy and was sold into slavery by them. In terms of family dynamics it would be difficult to find a more dramatic and hostile set of circumstances.

The competition between Esau and Jacob for their birthright, then, can be understood in generational terms. While it's true that their competitive spirit was

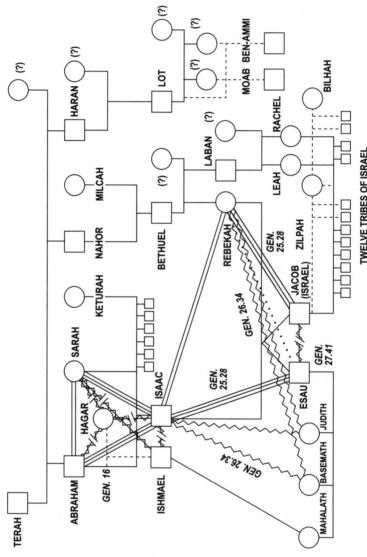

anticipated by the Lord (Gen. 25:23), what is also true is the generational pattern that was in place when they were born.

The explicit favoritism by the parents toward their children provoked an explicit competition between the siblings. The pattern begun by Abraham and Sarah continued in at least the following three generations.

RELATIONAL CUT-OFFS

In order to understand Jacob's anxiety as he anticipated his confrontation with Esau, let's focus upon a second generational pattern which is very much a part of the family story.

"If you don't like someone in your family, cut him/her off and drive him/her out." That had happened between Sarah and Hagar, between Isaac and Ishmael, and it happened between Jacob and Esau. The pattern of cutting people off when angry with them had begun years earlier with Jacob's grandparents, Abraham and Sarah.

Because of Sarah's infertility, she convinced (perhaps manipulated) Abraham into having a child by her servant Hagar (Gen. 16 ff.). Historically, multiple marriages were customary in Abraham's day, and it was commonplace for the handmaiden of a senior wife also to be the concubine to the husband. This kind of arrangement between Abraham and Hagar produced a son, Ishmael.

Sarah's naïveté led her to believe that the pressure she felt to produce a son for Abraham would be lifted if he had an heir by someone other than her. In fact, the exact opposite occurred. Hagar's fertility served only to highlight Sarah's barrenness. In much the same way that adoption doesn't solve a woman's feelings about the infertility in her marriage, so giving Abraham an heir by Hagar didn't solve Sarah's feelings about her infertility. Rather, it exacerbated them.

Before we go further, we need to read a bit between the lines of Scripture. One can't help wondering about Abraham and Sarah's marriage at this juncture. Just how did it make Sarah feel when Abraham apparently and willingly accepted her solution to the problem of her infertility? When a spouse goes outside the marriage, it is always very difficult, even traumatic, for the other partner, and sometimes fatal for their relationship. To return to our story, God had promised Abraham to make a great nation of his progeny, involving a male heir, presumably by Sarah (Gen. 15:4-5). Certainly Abraham and Sarah had talked about it, probably every month. God's promise wasn't a mystery to Sarah. It certainly wasn't a surprise to Abraham.

What did come as a surprise was Sarah's solution. Abraham would "lie with Hagar." How often, we don't know, but it's reasonable to believe that it happened many times. How did Sarah feel when Abraham agreed to take Hagar as his concubine? What would have motivated her to make such a suggestion? How did she feel each time she saw Hagar slip into Abraham's tent?

We think that Abraham in his typically passive way was able to communicate to Sarah that *their* problem was really *her* problem. Whatever humiliation she suffered, she probably suffered in silence. Abraham's choices couldn't have made Sarah feel good about herself or about Abraham, for that matter.

Sarah's strategy worked. Hagar became pregnant by Abraham, and Ishmael was born, further complicating the relationship between Sarah and Hagar. The difficulties in their relationship continued to fester for the next thirteen or fourteen years.

So, fourteen years after Hagar had conceived and borne Abraham a son, Sarah miraculously conceived and Isaac was born.

Unfortunately, Abraham's passivity appeared again in his family when, after Isaac's birth, Sarah turned against both Hagar and Ishmael and made scapegoats of them because of her resentful feelings toward them (Gen. 21:9 ff.). Ishmael was fourteen years old when Isaac was born. A bond had apparently formed between Abraham and Ishmael during those years, a bond that Sarah resented.

The text says that when Isaac was approximately two years old, old enough to have been weaned, Sarah happened upon Ishmael at a time when he was teasing Isaac. Our English text translates the word "mocking" but the Hebrew word is really better translated as "playing." Apparently he was teasing his younger half-brother. Maybe he was even being hostile. What older brother doesn't tease his younger brother hostilely at times? Whatever the reason, Sarah picked that occasion to force Abraham to make a terrible choice: between her and Hagar, between Isaac and Ishmael.

All we know from the biblical text is that the matter "distressed Abraham greatly" (Gen. 21:11). He had allowed an intolerable situation to develop over a period of at least fourteen years.

Imagine the many arguments Sarah and Abraham must have had about the boys, about Hagar, about their relationship with one another. We can imagine how difficult, sensitive, and volatile these tangled family relationships were for each person.

Finally, the conflict erupts to the surface and the "solution" is for Hagar and Ishmael to be driven from Abraham's household into the desert. God promises Abraham and Hagar that he will take care of her and her son from that day forward. In fact, God promises to make of Ishmael a great nation as well (Gen. 21:18).

But consider this situation: A woman along with her son was banished from a family for having carried out a family request. She had made it possible for the family to have what it thought it wanted and in the way that family had chosen to have an heir. Then, when another son was born, it seemed that Hagar and Ishmael were an increasing embarrassment to Sarah. Or were they a reminder of Abraham's and Sarah's earlier imprudence and unbelief? Notice the solution: Hagar and Ishmael are required to suffer the consequences, to "pay the price" for the choices of Sarah and Abraham. Separation and dissolution seemed preferable to reaching a more equitable resolution for each person involved. As we hear this story, our hearts go out to Hagar and Ishmael. They have been cut off from Abraham's family and are never again restored. In family-therapy terms, the pattern of relational cut-off has been established.

What is of importance to subsequent generations (in this example, to Jacob's) is *how* the conflict that existed between the members of Abraham's household was processed. Don't forget, ultimately, the birth of Ishmael was Sarah's and Abraham's solution to a problem. Both Abraham and Sarah had colluded in the decision and then weren't willing to live with the consequences.

In a similar vein, one of Jacob's dysfunctional "birthmarks" in his generation was the result of the family generational pattern to cut off and drive out family members if they were in conflict with the system. The option of working out the situation between the parties involved apparently wasn't considered. Not until Jacob decided to confront his brother, Esau, was the pattern changed. This Jacob did in spite of his fear of him and because of his desire to return to the land of his father.

We cannot underestimate the determination it took for Jacob to challenge his family's generational patterns. Family cut-offs are difficult to overcome. It takes great courage and thorough preparation to reestablish contact with an estranged person, whether the estrangement occurred through separation, divorce, childhood adoption, the trauma of war, or family argument and violence.

PASSIVE MALES, OVERLY RESPONSIBLE FEMALES

A final observation on another of Jacob's "birthmarks" involves the presence in all three generations of a passive male and an overly responsible female. In today's vernacular we call this pattern "co-dependency."

Passive spouses seem to have the ability to convince their mates that the unhappiness inside them is really the fault of the other person. Perhaps this was so for Abraham and Sarah. If the other person (Sarah) would only change, then the spouse (in this case, Abraham) would be happy. It didn't work. Whatever was wrong between Abraham and Sarah wasn't solved by Sarah's interventions or by Abraham's passivity.

Sarah should have known better. She had been the victim of Abraham's self-serving passivity many times.

Early in the Genesis account (12:10 ff.) Abraham had convinced Sarah to lie about her marriage as a way for him to protect his own skin from Pharaoh's warriors. When confronted with the possibility that he would be killed and Sarah kidnapped, rather than call upon God for protection from his enemies and face the frightening consequences, Abraham lied to his assailants and got Sarah to go along with the scam. Only after God intervened directly with Pharaoh were Abraham and Sarah set free and allowed to go their own way unharmed. Abraham's passivity was documented in capital letters.

Ironically, the same pattern occurred years later when Abraham and Sarah were confronted by the armies of Abimelech (Gen. 20:1 ff.). Again, Abraham convinced Sarah to go along with a false story, that she was his sister, and Sarah complied.

Here is a classic case of co-dependency — a dependent, passive male, unwilling to care for himself, and the co-dependent female sacrificing herself for the sake of her spouse. We would quickly point out, however, that the pattern of co-dependency is not limited to one gender. A man can be the overly responsible partner to his dependent wife, as well. Unfortunately, this sword cuts both ways.

Sarah regularly took care of Abraham, not in the healthy, care-giving sense, but in the "taking-responsibility-for-another" sense of the word. Abraham successfully got Sarah to try to solve his problems for him rather than take responsibility for solving them himself. The ingenious outcome of this co-dependency is that the dependent partner can blame the overly responsible partner if things don't work out. "After all, it was my spouse's idea in the first place, wasn't it?"

GENERATIONAL ROOTS

The "passive male" syndrome shows up in the next generation with Isaac and Rebekah. In Genesis 26 we read another fascinating installment in this generational "birthmark" pattern of male passivity and self-preservation. In this story Isaac is faced with a dilemma just like that which had confronted his father, Abraham. The writer of Genesis wants us to know that this incident occurs later than the story of Abraham because he writes, "Now there was a famine in the land *besides the previous famine that had occurred in the days of Abraham . . .*" (our emphasis). What happened to Isaac is clearly differentiated from what had happened to Abraham.

Isaac was confronted by Abimelech just as his father had been.*

Read the disquieting report of Isaac's passivity when faced by his adversary:

> When the men of the place asked about his wife, he said, "She is my sister." For he was afraid to say, "my wife," thinking, "the men of the place might kill me on account of Rebekah, for she is beautiful" (Gen. 26:7).

Like father, like son. The story is the same, as are the results. Rather than trust in God as his protector and live with the consequences, Isaac opts for the lie, a lie that requires collusion between himself and Rebekah. Likewise, as in the case of Abraham and the earlier Abimelech, God intervenes and protects Isaac and Rebekah. Their passivity and co-dependency flow together

---

* Whether the word translated "Abimelech" refers to the same person who confronted Abraham or whether it refers to a royal title is uncertain; biblical commentators are divided on the matter. What matters here is Isaac's response.

into a "birthmark" that continues to imprint itself on successive generations.

When the pattern finally arrives in Jacob's generation, it is full blown. As a young male, Jacob is dominated by his stronger, more manipulative mother. For example, when it came time for Isaac, as the patriarch, to bless his eldest son (a normal custom in the Near East), Rebekah is seen coaching Jacob. She tells him what to say, what to think, and what to do. The picture is one of a compliant son obeying his bossy and strong-willed mother (see Gen. 27).

Customarily we focus on Esau's irreverence in the story of the stolen blessing (Gen. 27:30 ff.). Certainly his behavior was destructive and unacceptable. His approach to his father's blessing is casual at best and irreverent at worst.

But, for purposes of our discussion, we want to focus upon the interplay between Rebekah and Isaac. We know little about their relationship except to note that Rebekah, in coaching Jacob to deceive Isaac, deliberately defied Isaac's patriarchal authority. Thus, the narrative supports the validity of Esau's anger toward Jacob, especially in light of the meaning attached to the ancient practice of the patriarch's blessing.

This part of the story ends with Jacob as a young man fleeing the wrath of his brother and going to his uncle's home in a distant land.

Generationally, this family functions without a tradition of a strong male as family patriarch. Rather, strong women take responsibility for keeping the family together and trying to make people happy. The men tend to do as they are told, or respond passively to situations. The resulting pattern is an unhealthy generational "birthmark," the kind of deformity that destroys the ability of the family to deal with conflict.

DECIDING TO BE DIFFERENT

Then comes the older Jacob. After fifteen or more years in exile, Jacob decides to return to the land of his father, a land still occupied by Esau, his assumed-to-be hostile and relationally cut-off brother. What happens as a result of his decision to return is what defines Jacob as a transitional person. In two very distinctive ways, Jacob is different from either Abraham or Isaac.

In terms of his decision not to be plagued by the passivity of his ancestors, the story in Genesis 32 is pertinent. It is the story that describes the event leading to Jacob's name being changed from Jacob to Israel. It describes how *Jacob learned to struggle and wrestle with God.*

Most biblical commentators believe the "man" who wrestled with Jacob was a theophany, the appearance of God in human form. During their conflict, it's clear that Jacob realized the stature and status of his antagonist because he insists that the man "bless" him. The man responds by asking Jacob his name. When Jacob tells him his name, the man responds with the following words: "Your name shall no longer be Jacob, but Israel; for you have striven with God and with men and have prevailed." Jacob's response to the event demonstrates its significance to him: "So Jacob called the place Peniel, saying, 'It is because I saw God face to face and yet my life was spared'" (Gen. 32:30).

What a story. Somehow, Jacob had learned to fight for what he believed in, to state what he wanted, to wrestle with difficulty, to take action, to persevere, to hold on and prevail. Only when Jacob's generational history of male passivity is taken into account is the significance of the blessing by Jacob's antagonist fully revealed. In wrestling with God, Jacob learned to function differently than either his father or his grandfather. Jacob had learned to struggle with God and God blessed him for it.

Looking back, we are able to see how much could have changed for the better if Abraham and Sarah had wrestled with God when they were faced with personal danger and the dilemma of not having a child of their own.

Certainly Abraham and Isaac could have wrestled with God and not have subjugated their wives to the humiliation of their experiences in another man's household. And certainly Abraham could have "striven" with Sarah, first when she suggested his liaison with Hagar, and subsequently in her insistence on cutting off Hagar and Ishmael and driving them out. Likewise, Sarah could have struggled with God over her barrenness rather than resorting to her manipulative means.

What does it mean "to struggle and wrestle with God"? Is it right? Is it proper?

The example of Jesus in the Garden of Gethsemane the night before his crucifixion is the classic example of what to wrestle with God about and how to wrestle with Him. Jesus' struggle was evident. His agony was real. His ambivalence was clear. He didn't want to go through what the next few days held in store.

Jesus' struggle with God involved the same kind of life-threatening issues as those faced by the Patriarchs—the impending danger of a hostile crowd, the emptying of his place of privilege as the Son, the blind abandonment to the will of his Father. Whatever the net effect, Jesus knew how to wrestle with God, and it was appropriate for him to do so.

Jacob became Israel because he chose to begin to remove the debilitating "birthmarks" that had plagued his family for generations. He had learned not to be carried along by life as if things were out of his control. He had learned to relate to God as if his opinion mattered. He was a person, created in the image of God. He was not an automaton. And he was bold enough to bring that relationship to the table in his striving with God.

The second decision Jacob made was *to be reconciled to his brother* (Gen. 32-33). After years of alienation from Esau, Jacob made the decision to return to the land of his fathers even though the decision necessitated a difficult and possibly dangerous confrontation.

Given the generational anxiety undergirding the story, Jacob's action takes on even greater meaning. He was the first to find his way home. Jacob's elaborate scheme in preparation for his meeting with Esau only underlined Jacob's anxiety. Jacob expected to be killed. Perhaps he even deserved it.

Yet, we are told that when the two brothers came together, "Esau ran to meet him and embraced him, and fell on his neck and kissed him, and they wept" (Gen. 33:4).

In his anxiety Jacob expected the worst. God's grace allowed for the best. The generational pattern of the family presaged continued alienation. Jacob's willingness to take the risk of returning opened the possibility for reconciliation. Thus, the family story was changed.

While it is important to prepare for the worst, as Jacob did, when taking the initiative to bring about reconciliation, it is also important to prepare for, even hope for, a positive response.

CONCLUDING THOUGHTS

It's clear, then, that our relationship with God does not exempt us from relational and generational patterns. Certainly, in the case of Abraham, Sarah, Isaac, Rebekah, and even the young Jacob, the family's generational history was a strong influence. While they are "examples of faith," they are also examples of how family generational patterns may transcend traditional spiritual categories. Being a transitional person, as was the mature, older Jacob, involves looking beyond traditional religious solutions to family problems. Generational "birthmarks" are passed on almost as if there were a genetically coded method for doing so. Of course there isn't, but we must understand and be able to recognize what the patterns are in our own family.

The men and women of the Bible were very human, influenced by tradition, culture, and family history and expectations. Then, as now, it was difficult to know how to be faithful to God, oneself, and one's family. Indeed, it often required "wrestling" with God and coping with the anxiety of that process.

Like Jacob, we can learn to strive and to wrestle with God. The paradox of the solution is in the admission that only God can ultimately change what needs to be changed. Yet, in the same way, we are told to "work out our own salvation with fear and trembling" (Phil. 2:12). God expects each of us to be an active participant in the story rather than a passive observer. The good news is that God is willing to engage Himself with us, even struggle with us, in the process. He, more than we, is interested in the outcome. It is possible that God would have more of us challenge Him so that our names are changed, like Jacob, to "Israel." Transitional people are the ones who have striven with God and with men and have prevailed.

5.

"What's a Mother to Do?"

The commercial that spawned this chapter title was intended to send the message that "mothers are responsible for mostly everything in the lives of their children." The commercial shows a mother, her face wrinkled with concern, carrying the weight of her anxiety for her sick child on her shoulders while asking the audience to support her because of her fear. The purpose of the commercial is clearly to use a mother's apprehension for her child as a means of selling the sponsor's product. Every mother who feels ultimate responsibility for her children is a candidate for the commercial's message: as the primary caretakers of the family they ought to buy whatever the advertiser is selling in order to carry out their motherly responsibilities.

While commercials usually emphasize how material things can help mothers and fathers become good parents, the term "mothering" actually refers to a process involving care-giving, comfort-giving and encouragement, usually by the female but sometimes by others.* Thus, this chapter on "mothering" is addressed to *all* primary care-givers and parents, grandparents, nannies, foster or adoptive parents.

A MOTHER'S LOVE

"Mothering" begins with care-giving. By this we mean the provision of physical and emotional nurture.

In his classic book *The Art of Loving*, the psychologist Erich Fromm wrote of a mother's love, or care-giving, as having two dimensions. According to Fromm, they are best described by the metaphors of "milk" and "honey." Milk has to do with the provision of essential physical care such as the changing of dirty diapers, the preparation of food, and the furnishing of support and a safe environment, etc. Most mothers are motivated and work very hard to provide this kind of care.

On the other hand, "honey," says Fromm, has to do with the provision of the sweetness of life, the celebration of being alive, of being a person. Thus, honey

---

* For a more detailed discussion of the issue of mothering from our perspective, see Nancy Chodorow, *The Reproduction of Mothering: Psychoanalysis and the Sociology of Gender* (Berkeley, CA: University Press, 1978). In addition, our thinking about the mother-child relationship itself has been greatly influenced by the writings of Mary Ainsworth (cf. *Patterns of Attachment* [New York: Erlbaum Publishers, 1978]; and Daniel Stern, *The Interpersonal World of the Infant* [New York: Basic Books, 1985]).

includes the birthday parties a child remembers when he or she grows up; the costumes stitched to wear to school for a Halloween parade; the experience of being taught to ride your very own bike without the training wheels. "Honey" is laughter. The French call it "le joie de vivre," the joy of living.

In a recent discussion with our eldest daughter, Sheryl, she reflected upon the "honey" in her life as a child. According to Sheryl, Dennis "mothered" her by reading to her (especially the C. S. Lewis series *The Chronicles of Narnia*) and by telling stories complete with sound effects and vocal accents. She can still recreate, almost verbatim, the stories Dennis told more than fifteen years ago.

Lucy was the more pervasive "mother." For example, both of our daughters remember with fondness the sweetness of exploring fields of milkweed and anise in search of caterpillars destined to become Monarch and Swallowtail butterflies. The three of them would bring the sprigs of green home, each with its captured larvae. They remember building the round cages of wire screen and placing the paper plates on top, then waiting to observe the mystery of metamorphosis.

Every time, on schedule, the miracle of life would unfold: first would come the insect's weaving of its chrysalis; next would be the wait until the hanging cylinder turned a dark, smoky green; and last would be the emerging of the damp-winged, fully formed butterfly. Carefully they would carry the container into the backyard and lift the paper plate from the screened top. Slowly, the miracle would be completed. The butterfly would sense its freedom, spread its wings, and fly off into the wind and sky while mother and daughters would watch, talk, and identify with the process that was being lived out before them.

The girls were like the butterflies. One day they would grow up and fly away. It was to be expected. The sweetness of the memories remains to this day. They are indeed precious, like honey.

After care-giving comes the process of comforting. Being mothered involves being held when you hurt and stroked when you're afraid.

We live in a frightening world. Life is neither safe nor is it fair. Hurt and pain are inevitable. Predictably, the smaller and less powerful you are, the more fearful you become. The mothering we refer to involves surrounding the child with the safe presence of the comfort-giver, in the midst of the hurt and at the time of the pain. It is the ointment and the soothing touch of succor. Comfort, most of all, is being listened to, being held up to be an important person worthy of being paid attention.*

Comfort is what we all need regularly at some time or another, however young or old we are.

The third dimension of mothering is encouragement. By this we mean the support of believing in someone even when he / she doesn't believe in or is unsure of him / herself. This cheer-leading function is well known to all parents of Little-Leaguers.

---

* We note the following quotation from Daniel Stern having to do with what he calls the process of "attunement": "Attuning behavior can be quite good even when your heart isn't in it. And as every parent knows, your heart can't always be in it, for all of the obvious reasons from fatigue through competing agendas to external preoccupations that fluctuate from day to day. Going through the motions is an expectable part of everyday parental experience. Attunements, then, vary along the dimension of authenticity, as well as of goodness of match." (*The Interpersonal World of the Infant*, p. 217).

The encouragement you receive is the support that prompts you to reach beyond yourself and to accomplish that at which you thought you would fail. It allows you to take risks and to find the boundaries of your abilities without feeling like a failure when you reach your limits.

TONY'S STORY

While Dennis has been trained as a marriage and family therapist, Lucy's specialty is student development. She has spent the last ten years working in the world of young adults, first as the Director of Student Concerns at Fuller Theological Seminary, and most recently as the Executive Director of the Caltech Y, an affiliate organization of the California Institute of Technology. Whenever we engage in dialogue about a particular issue she is forever prefacing her remarks with "that's what's so great about a developmental perspective . . . ." When she analyzes a human problem she automatically begins with a person's stage of development. She intuitively begins with mothering.

Such was the case when Tony walked into her office several years ago. Tony was in his last year of seminary, preparing for the ministry. He hadn't yet decided whether to pursue a pastoral call in a local parish setting or to seek an appointment as a missionary in his denomination's overseas operations. As their conversation unfolded, it was clear that Tony was struggling. He was confused as to the direction he should take. He couldn't make up his mind and was beating himself up psychologically because of it.

In line with her orientation, Lucy first sought to reassure him about his uncertainty because of his developmental stage. His stage of life, young adulthood, typically involves a time of reevaluation. As best as she could see, Tony was right on target.

Tony, however, wouldn't be comforted. "This problem is too familiar . . . . The decision is too important . . . . The pressure's too much . . . . The decision has got to be made. It's been put off too long." Tony seemed at the end of some kind of psychological rope.

They finished their conversation, Tony left the office and Lucy returned to her desk. Tony was right. Something was, indeed, different about his situation. Although they had talked for more than an hour, they were spinning their wheels. Somehow, Tony couldn't get his wheels to take hold on the career path he was seeking. The reasons behind his struggle were a mystery.

On the way home, a drive of less than fifteen minutes, a thought occurred to Lucy. In her questioning of Tony, as best she could remember, never once did he respond to one of her questions in the first person. That is, never once did he say "I want this" or "I like or don't like that." Every one of his answers was couched in the statements or opinions of others. He was totally focused on what others thought or felt. He thought in the third person, what others wanted him to do. When it came to himself, he found it virtually impossible to think in terms of what he might want or not want, like or not like.

Later that evening at home the conversation with Tony came up for discussion between us.

"Why wouldn't he be able to answer me in the first person?" Lucy asked.

"Maybe he can't," Dennis replied.

"Why?" she continued.

"You tell me. You're the developmental specialist."

(The verbal jousting between us with reference to our academic frames of reference sometimes comes out as sarcasm.)

But, Lucy wouldn't let go. Tony's problem was bothering her, and her next appointment with him was coming up in a few days. She needed a direction for their conversation.

The answer to her question finally popped to the surface in her mind. "Maybe he couldn't because he doesn't have a developed self. Maybe he can't form or express an opinion of his own because that part of his person has never developed. When does that part of a person begin to develop?"

Dennis reached back into his memories on the psychology of the self. "Very, very early. Probably in the first two years of life."

Lucy tucked the thought away and went on with the events of the evening.

Two days later, Tony kept his appointment in her office. After the usual preliminary pleasantries, Lucy broached the subject. "Tony, I couldn't help noticing after our last conversation that every time I asked you what you wanted, your answer was always couched in terms of what others wanted you to do. Do you ever have an opinion for yourself, especially when it comes to yourself?"

Her line of questioning caught him off guard. "Well, of course I do," he stammered.

"Then tell me one. Tell me one thing about your future that would represent something you would want or would like to do." She wanted him to respond in the first person. The request seemed straightforward. Supposedly easy.

Tony's response was classic. He sat in the chair across from her and said nothing. He wasn't being stubborn. She could tell from the look on his face. He was confused. "I don't know. It's never occurred to me. I just don't think like that."

Not one opinion, not one thought of his own. No wonder he couldn't think about the future. It was as if he really didn't exist except as an expression of someone else's ideas about him. Tony didn't have a developed self, or at least, if one did exist it was so weak and unconscious to Tony so as not to be easily identified or expressed.

Lucy's relationship with Tony had to begin at the very beginning. He needed mothering.

A RIGHT TO EXIST

In the weeks that followed, Tony's "birthmark" became more clear. He had experienced significant maternal neglect and deprivation.

When he was a very young child, between the ages of one and two, his mother became pregnant with his sister. Early in her pregnancy she began to hemorrhage and the family doctor was afraid she would lose the baby. As a result he sent her to bed. For the next six months it was as if Tony didn't have a mother while she focused upon keeping her fetus alive.

The father did what he could, but he worked full time to support the family, and according to the stories Tony was told, the father was unable to do all that needed to get done. He was barely able to care for his one-year-old son. Tony survived a series of child-care arrangements, but that was all.

When it came near the time for the new baby to be delivered, the infant arrived prematurely, and for the next six months the whole family, especially the mother, focused on Tony's newborn sister.

In the process Tony got "lost." He was not the kind of child who caused problems even as a baby. He just disappeared into the woodwork. He learned to play by himself in his crib for hours at a time. He learned not to make demands. He learned to live in the margins of his family. The pattern persisted throughout his years as a child and as an adolescent and into his young adulthood.

Tony's new baby sister was exactly the opposite. She lived in the center of the family. She yelled and screamed from the day she was brought home from the hospital. She had learned to assert her presence in the hospital where the nurses were at her beck and call, and she continued to do so when her mother became her primary care-giver at home.

In fact, as the years went by, the sister increasingly became the center of her mother's world, doing all the things as a child and as an adolescent that the mother had never been allowed to do for herself as a child.

When Tony and his sister made the transition into young adulthood, Tony kept on performing his cooperative role in the family to the hilt. He had never caused his parents a single problem or moment of concern in his entire life.

Symbolically, when he graduated from high school his family forgot to bring the camera, so there were no pictures. The same thing happened when he graduated from college, with honors but no celebration.

The only bright spot he could remember was that he had found some sense of meaning in the church he and his parents attended, leading him to decide, without much forethought, to seek a career in ministry. The church was the one place where he felt he most belonged.

In contrast to Tony's pattern, his younger sister continued to dominate her parents' lives even as an adult. In her college years she had developed an addiction to marijuana and had dropped out of school, requiring a time of hospitalization. Her treatment for drugs had not worked, and, according to Tony, she was now married to her second husband, a man her parents feared was involved in the drug trade. They had loaned his sister thousands of dollars for bail money to get the husband out of jail. They were resentful and felt trapped. The parents just couldn't say no.

MAKING EXCUSES

What happened next is typical in situations such as Tony's. Every time Lucy would bring up the possibility of his being neglected as a child, he would try to explain away his parents' behaviors, especially his mother's. Usually the excuses would take the form of "she did the best she knew how" or "she really never meant to neglect me." And again, "Why can't I just forget the past, forgive her, and move on?"

Tony didn't realize it, but the kind of parent/child relationship he had experienced is one of the most difficult of all to work through. Its difficulty lies in the subtle nature of neglect. In the case of *parental abuse*, the child has memories, typically painful, of incidents that he or she can remember. The memories, though bad, form the substance or the outline for forgiveness.

In the case of *parental neglect*, there is no substance, only a vacuum. Somehow it's more difficult to forgive what *didn't* happen than to forgive what did happen.

Lucy's strategy was to support Tony's right to exist and his right to have an opinion of his own. She listened to him, and encouraged him to identify his feelings, even when the feelings weren't appropriate according to his family's rules. He had to learn how to be angry before he could let himself be angry about something. He had to allow himself the right to be angry before he could release the anger through forgiveness. He had to become a person in order to find the self within him.

A THREE-LEGGED STOOL

The key concept that seemed to unlock the process of self-development for Tony was a metaphor viewing the Great Commandment as a three-legged stool. The Great Commandment referred to in the Gospels is "You shall love the Lord your God with all your heart, and with all your soul, and with all your strength, and with all your mind; and your neighbor as yourself" (Luke 10:27, NASB).

The first leg of the stool is to love God. The second is to love yourself, and the third is to love your neighbor. The "three-leggedness" of the commandment is what gives love stability, or equilibrium.

Some people, however, who verbally advocate loving God and loving their neighbor find it difficult to advocate loving themselves. Why? Because in some quarters loving yourself has come to be thought of as selfishness. This approach might suggest that Tony's sister "loved herself" too much.

In fact, quite the opposite was true.

Neither Tony nor his sister was effectively mothered. Tony wasn't, because he was neglected. That's easy to see. The case of his sister is harder to recognize.

As Lucy explained it to Tony, when his mother and father made his sister the center of their world, they robbed his sister of her right to be a normal child. Though it may have felt good to be their child at the time, his sister suffered because she, in an upside-down kind of way, became a means to her parent's ends. The sister was spoiled in order to make the mother feel good about herself, and the father colluded in the process. The girl gave the mother a reason to exist and in the process lost her own independent reason to be a person.

Whenever parents turn their world inside out and orbit around their children rather than expecting the children to adapt to them, the children will suffer accordingly. They lose the freedom of being children, of being irresponsible, irrepressible, and incorrigible, as is the nature of children at times. The child's position, being at the center of the parent's world, is oppressive. While it feels good to the child at the time, the process leads to bondage. It's a sad thing to lose the freedom to be a child in deference to taking care of a parent's still unresolved childhood needs.

Loving yourself, then, involves learning to "mother yourself." The axiom would be "As you were mothered, so it is that you will love yourself." Most typically, the ability of a person to love her / himself is based upon her / his experience of being mothered. That's what mothering does. The mothering acts like a mirror in which the child first experiences her / himself as a person.

When that love is secure, the child is able eventually to focus on others. That is, he / she is able to learn to love his / her neighbor. When that love is not secure, however, the child may focus upon her / himself to the exclusion of God or her / his neighbor (as was the case of Tony's sister). Or, he / she may focus upon loving

God or his / her neighbor more. That is, the child will lengthen the legs on the stool because the leg marked "loving yourself" has been shortened.

In Tony's case, he tried to solve his dilemma by lengthening the leg marked "loving God." His strategy worked, up to a point. It worked until the day-to-day realities of his life put him in contact with people who needed something from him and he had few resources to give. That was what lay beneath his paralysis. He unconsciously knew that his choice of ministry, whether in the parish or on the mission field, would take him into contact with people who would need something from him. In order to minister to them he would have to have a developed self, to be a person, a foundation from which to give. His self was lacking and he was scared.

On the other hand, some people who don't know how to love themselves, try to lengthen the "loving neighbor" leg. In the previous chapter we referred to these folk as being co-dependent.

They make it their lifetime work to take care of others, often to their own hurt and injury. They become professional "mothers." Sometimes they take pleasure in being taken advantage of, in "loving too much." They are the martyrs of the family. Their martyrdom means that their sacrifice is all that more significant, and if it's significant, it means that they have worth.

Last of all are the folk who try to love themselves and their neighbors to the exclusion of loving God. Through their behavior, loving God becomes human-ism or some other religion focused upon humankind. Whatever form it takes, the leg on the stool marked "loving God" is shortened, and their view of the world lacks vertical dimension. Life is lived instead on a horizontal plane. Great good can be done, but the Godward dimension is missing.

A FINAL WORD

We are suggesting that you begin your own journey where the Bible begins. In the first chapter of the Book of Genesis it is written that the Spirit "hovered" or "brooded" over the surface of the waters as God anticipated the acts of creation. The hovering and brooding described the process of mothering in which the Godhead engaged as the earth and the skies were formed.

In terms of your own life, your own childhood, the childhood of those you love, the childhoods of the generations that preceded you, *what patterns of mothering do you observe?* Allow a sense of the process to develop in your consciousness.

Next, *remember from your own experience the examples of mothering* that seem to be relevant to your reflection. And, last of all, *think through the implications of your discoveries.* What can you learn about yourself, your mother, or your primary care-giver? To what must you "attune" yourself as you begin to listen to yourself? Allow the agenda of your own generations to begin to emerge.

6.

What Do Fathers Do?

When Dennis was seven years old, his father died two weeks after his return from serving in North Africa during World War II. Dennis's mother never remarried, so he grew up as an only child of a single parent. With his father's death, life changed forever. Most of all, Dennis had to learn how to grow up without a father.

For example, learning to shave is a fairly normal experience for most boys. Typically, they observe their father's daily ritual over a period of years and are then prepared when they decide it's time to shave their peach fuzz. For a boy-child of a widowed, single parent, it's not that easy.

In Dennis's case he decided to shave one morning when he was about thirteen.

He went into the bathroom, closed the door (locked it, of course), and reached for his mother's Gillette razor, the kind that opens the head of the razor by twisting the bottom of the handle. The only problem was that Dennis didn't realize he needed to twist the base of the razor to tighten the head. As a result, the much-used double-edged blade lay loosely in its head rather than being held in place by the tightened handle.

He lathered up, spread the shaving cream on his face, looking at himself in the mirror with pride, and with all the masculine gusto he could muster he took the first swath at his peach-fuzzed face. Unfortunately, the razor, with its dull, loose double blade, wobbled across his face, gouging the skin as he pulled.

"Shaving is tougher than I thought," he muttered.

He dutifully continued this masculine ritual, managing to scrape off several patches of his facial epidermis as he went. When he finished, his face was a checkered, bleeding mass.

He wondered, "Now, what do I do with this mess?"

"That's what shaving lotion must be for," he thought, reaching for an old bottle of his grandfather's Mennen Aftershave. Because the bleeding was so profuse, he figured he needed a lot of lotion, so he splashed his palm with the astringent liquid and slathered it generously on his wounds. Needless to say, his face ignited in pain as the wounds and the aftershave came into contact.

Through tear-filled eyes, he decided that shaving was rough indeed and that perhaps he would put it off until he was older — much older. He dabbed his wounds with a towel, layered his face with bits of toilet paper, unlocked the door, and sheepishly returned to the real world believing that being a man was tougher than he thought. In fact, he believed he must be a sissy because doing what men traditionally do was so hard for him. He didn't realize that what he lacked was the special knowledge learned from a role model. He didn't lack courage or manliness.

Writing this chapter was another reminder of the dilemma Dennis faced growing up. We'll explain:

Our custom is for Dennis to take the first swing at writing at the word processor, with Lucy editing the copy copiously, as needed. When it came time to write this chapter, Dennis hit a wall. Weeks passed without his being able to write. Writer's block became a present reality rather than a distant concept.

Finally, after much soul-searching, he realized that our chapter on mothering should logically be followed by a chapter on fathering, a process he had never really, personally experienced. Although he had fathered two grown daughters, and had read several books on the subject, he had never himself been fathered. Fathering someone else is different from being fathered oneself.

Single-parent families like Dennis's are a significant reality in the United States. In fact, current statistics suggest that 50 percent of all children under the age of eighteen will spend a significant amount of time, probably several years, in a single-parent household.

Shared custody, alternating residences, step-parenting, child care by extended family members or child-care centers are the norm for many children. "Fathering" is for many men as confusing, mysterious, and tough as Dennis's first shaving experience.

In the past three decades Americans have "remade their society" and are left with many concerns and questions and few answers. For example, a recent Gallup Poll, published by *Newsweek* magazine, indicated the following concerns:

—49 percent of Americans thought the American family to be worse off today than it was ten years ago. 39 percent thought it to be better off.
—The participants in the poll split evenly, 42 percent vs. 42 percent, as to whether they thought the American family would be better off ten years from now.
—68 percent thought it important for a family to make some financial sacrifices so that one parent could stay home to raise the children. In contrast, 27 percent thought it best to have both parents working so the family could benefit from the highest possible income.*

The essence of *Newsweek*'s concern is clearly with how we as a people will adapt to our changing culture and how that adaptation will affect our children. The concern focuses upon the twin processes of parenting: mothering and fathering.

For more and more families, these parenting roles are shared by both men and women, especially the "fathering" role as we understand it. The pressure is particularly great for the woman in the family. She is often expected to do double duty, or necessarily work a "second shift."**

* *Newsweek*, "The 21st Century Family," Special Edition, Winter/Spring, 1990.
** For an excellent discussion of the implications of the woman's dilemma see *The Second Shift: Inside the Two-Job Family* by Arlie Hochschild and Anne Machung (New York: Penguin Press, 1989).

FATHERING INVOLVES PROVISION

Historically, stereotypes of male and female roles in America have been that men are the "providers" or "breadmakers" for the family and women are the "homemakers" or "bread bakers." Although the latter is almost always true, the former is no longer the case for many families. Women earn money outside the home and, more often than not, their income is necessary for the sustenance of the family. Two-paycheck families, if not two-career families, represent the norm.

This shouldn't surprise us. It has been true for most families throughout the world and throughout history. If men were the hunters, women were the gatherers. In the largest countries in the world today, for example, China and India, women are expected to work outside the home as well as in the home. Few families have the option of having a wife and mother whose sole responsibility it is to be at home and to take care of the family.

What's more important for families is whether or not the provisional needs of the family are met sufficiently in a steady and stable manner. This is the reason most women with children give for working outside the home. Provisional needs involve material goods. Obvious needs such as food, water, and shelter fall into the category of provisional needs. Families also need the provision of an adequate diet, appropriate clothing, the ability to get to and from school and activities, medical and dental care, and a warm place to sleep, that is, the physical care most often provided by the income of a working parent.

What seems to be hard on children is an unstable and inconsistent provisional environment. Such is the case with the family of an alcoholic or addicted parent. Whether or not the bills will be paid, whether or not there will be food in the refrigerator, whether or not the rent will be met—these are the terrifying, overarching questions facing many families. That survival itself is in doubt is especially difficult. Families in general, and children in particular, need to know, to be certain, that their physical environment is adequate.

FATHERING INVOLVES PROTECTION

The second dimension of fathering involves protection or safety, both in the physical and emotional sense of the term.

Home, whether you're a child or an adult, single or married, living alone or in community, should feel like a secure place in which to be. We all want a safe place to come back to.

Fathering also includes physically protecting a family. Warding off physical danger is more than important. It's sometimes necessary.

Several years ago our family was in San Francisco for a wedding. We had brunch in a downtown hotel and were walking to our car when we looked across the street and saw a disheveled man walking toward us. Without warning, he began to make suggestive and vulgar comments to the women in our group. Dennis remembers feeling that he was going to have to fight the guy and that he would ruin his good suit.

As the man circled the family, we huddled together, much like a wagon train under siege by Indians. The man continued muttering obscenities as we waited for the violence to begin. Then suddenly, without further harassing us, the man turned and walked on. We looked at each other and collectively breathed a sigh of relief. Shannon, our youngest daughter, broke the silence.

"Boy, it's a good thing you're so big, Dad. We were all able to hide behind you." With that comment we all laughed and our tension was released. Then, each of us told the others what we had planned to do if the man had attacked. Lucy was ready to hit him with her spiked-heel shoe. The girls were ready to pummel him and run for help. Dennis had prepared himself for a fist fight. The danger had risen like an angry sea and had passed without harming any of us. We were safe. We felt protected. We went on to the wedding and enjoyed the rest of the day with some measure of unity, even though we had not actually needed to fend off the potential danger. We had been ready. Each of us had prepared to "father" those we loved, to protect one another as needed.

Our need for emotional security is as great as for physical safety, although it often goes unrecognized. Occasionally, someone in the family will have to say, "Now. Now. Let's all settle down before someone gets hurt. This fight has gone far enough." A family needs someone to function as its barometer and thermometer, monitoring its highs and the lows, staying in touch with the family temperature.

Occasionally a line that means "this has gone far enough" needs to be drawn. Emotional security is knowing that the violence which is in you and in those whom you love will be contained. Of course, in any family there are occasional outbursts of anger, heated emotions, and minor conflicts of everyday life. Emotional security is rooted in the confidence that anger is not more powerful than love, that conflict can be resolved, that differences of opinion are to be expected and can be worked through. Fathering involves sometimes taking initiative to bring about confrontation as well as restoration, understanding, and forgiveness.

FATHERING INVOLVES DIRECTION

A primary aspect of the fathering function we're calling "direction" is the *provision of a world view for the family.* By world view we mean a perspective on life, a way of looking at people and things, and a means of interpreting reality.

The free-enterprise incentive system, for example, is an American perspective, a world view essential to the "American" way of life. As a people, we benefit from capitalism's strengths and we are subject to its weaknesses — its acquisitive, materialistic, and consumer-based thinking.

Christianity too has a "world view." Unfortunately, contemporary understanding of the word *Christian* and the world view it supposedly represents, has robbed it of its essence as describing a follower of Jesus Christ, with all that implies, and now limits it to shallow or abstract ideological implications. "Christians" are at war with Muslims in Beirut. "Christians" are at war with one another in Northern Ireland. Christianity perceived as an ideology has failed.

In contrast, a follower of Christ is one who attempts to live above contemporary ideologies, deciding to walk among people as Christ walked among them. Being a Christian includes accepting what he accepted and hating what he hated. To be a follower of Christ is to walk in Jesus' steps and to love and live among others as he loved and lived. This may include suffering persecution as he suffered and bearing a cross as he bore his.

Every family needs a "father" who establishes the world view or direction the family will go. Our hope is that he will echo the words of Joshua, "As for me and my house, we will serve the Lord," where following Jesus Christ is more than an ideology. Rather, for him and his family it is a way of life.

A second dimension of "direction" is the *gyroscopic function of fathering*. A gyroscopic compass is a highly accurate, reliable navigational aid, always indicating true north, unaffected by the earth's magnetic field and unaffected by the pitching and rolling of whatever vehicle is carrying it. So also, a family needs a person whose value system allows the family to be centered. When a gyroscope is working, the vehicle carrying it is capable of operating on autopilot because it will be kept steady with relation to the horizon. In the moving and shifting world in which we live it's difficult to find the horizon, let alone orient ourselves to it. "Fathering" is the ability to provide a fixed and steady center based upon a clearly defined value system that allows the members of a family to determine where they are with reference to the past, present, and the future.

Another metaphor for the idea is to visualize it as the center pole of the tent which holds the rest of the pieces of the tent together. In his letter in the New Testament, James writes that a characteristic of wisdom that is from above is "unwavering" (3:17). The Greek word used by James denotes a center pole, or something like a gyroscope. It signifies the unfaltering quality of a mature follower of Christ who is anchored to the reality of God rather than tethered to the changing, ambiguous appearances of life. Families need the stability of an "unwavering" center.

Another dimension of the idea of "direction" is *gatekeeping*. Tevye, the Russian Jewish father in the musical *Fiddler on the Roof*, comes to mind as an example of what we mean. Tevye believes it is his duty to protect and preserve his family's Jewish traditions. One of these traditions is to make certain that his daughters marry within the faith of their fathers. The poignant moment of the musical is when a young and handsome gentile Communist revolutionary captures the love and affection of Tevye's daughter. She chooses to follow him and leaves her family. Tevye's agony is his perceived failure as the gatekeeper of the family. How can he find a way of accepting her choice of a husband?

Families need fathering. They need gatekeepers whose wisdom preserves the history or story of the family, while at the same time it releases the members of the family to be their own persons. Such is the task of the one who "sits at the gate."

The final aspect of direction is *discipline*. The Greek word most often used in Scripture to describe this function is *paideia* It is used in both the Old and New Testaments to describe the role of the father (cf. Prov. 1:8 and Eph. 6:4). The word connotes a pruning action whose purpose it is to direct the growth of a plant or tree. Discipline is the behavior of a parent intended to control the behaviors of a child, within a context of love. By definition, the word precludes acts of hostility and abuse. It includes acts of control and purpose.

Most important, discipline involves creating a relational climate in which what is physically external (i.e., physical discipline) is safely internalized (i.e., self-discipline). The physical limits and boundaries set by the parent are internalized and become the inner limits and boundaries of the child's conscience.

When the loop is completed, *paideia* is self-perpetuating and self-generating. The child learns to parent her/himself.

For example, Dennis recently had a conversation with a young father about an experience he had had in trying to get his four-year-old son to clean up his room. Typically, his son, as the baby of the family, would wander around while his two older siblings cleaned the room for him. It had become a pattern. When the father intervened, the youngest son "pitched a fit" (the father's words).

Ordinarily, the father would have spanked his son and the boy would have wailed uncontrollably for hours, never cleaning the room. Every time before, the boy had been able to thwart the will of his parents by throwing a tantrum, with someone else picking up after him.

This time, the father decided that his son didn't really understand what "cleaning your room" meant. So, he walked the boy through the process, step by step. "First, you pick up your toys and put them in the box. Next, you hang up your clothes and put them in the closet, but put the dirty ones in the hamper. Then, you pull the covers up to the top of the mattress and make your bed," and so forth. He insisted that his son clean his room and he gave him the skills to do so, communicating that they were not going to leave the bedroom until the task was finished.

The child has been doing his share of the work in cleaning his room ever since. The father insisted that his son obey him, gave him the skills and support to do so, and changed the way he related to and disciplined his son.

FATHERING INCLUDES EMPOWERMENT

The *final function of fathering is empowerment:* the ability to create a context within which a child is able to reach his or her potential and to acquire the character and skills needed to be self-reliant.

The concept is close to that of discipline; however, the key thought is "self-reliance." We've chosen this idea rather than the more common ideas of independence and autonomy for a specific reason. We'll explain.

In the summers of 1986 and 1987 it was our privilege to spend several weeks ministering in the East African countries of Kenya and Uganda. We were introduced to the cultural differences between our respective countries. One of the differences had to do with how and when a young person is determined to be an adult.

In America, with its rampant individualism, we emphasize the ability of a young person to function independently of his or her family, to act as an autonomous person. In Kenya the idea of independence is subordinated to the idea of self-reliance. And, self-reliance is defined as *the ability of the person to come alongside the other adults in the community and to shoulder a fair share of the weight and responsibility for the community.* Their idea of self-reliance has responsibility built into it. The American concept of independence doesn't. Thus, we celebrate our young when they have traveled on their own through Europe backpacking as they go. They trek autonomously, separate from us.

In Kenya, such trekking is seen as just another stage of dependence, perhaps a more advanced stage, but still dependence. In their eyes, a young person hasn't become a full adult until he or she returns to the community and takes up a fair share of responsibility for the community. While it is true that an adult may travel to the city to work, the connection with the home community is still felt; the responsibility is still acknowledged.

Every family needs someone who empowers others to reach their potential, while at the same time they remain connected to the home base.

To empower is to expect more from these persons than they can comfortably achieve, yet to accept what they are actually able to do even if it doesn't quite meet hoped-for standards. To empower is to lend your weight and influence at critical times when your loved ones are discouraged or blocked. To empower is to help them cut through the maze of fears, anxieties, or confusion which binds them. To empower is to believe that they can do the job. You disempower them if you do the job for them. To empower is to encourage them to become your equal and to stand aside when they are your equal and you know that they will surpass you. To empower is not to be threatened nor jealous of their success, but to bless them.

We want to leave you with two concluding thoughts about empowerment.

The first has to do with the difference between empowerment and enablement. To enable a person is to perpetuate his / her dependency upon you by solving problems for him / her rather than allowing him / her to solve problems for him / herself. To enable is to shield a person from the consequences of her / his behaviors rather than letting her / him experience the natural consequences of her / his choices. Enablement subtly sends the message "you need me in order to live, to survive, to be successful." To enable is to disempower the person from achieving his / her potential and ever becoming your equal.

The second of our concluding thoughts about empowerment has to do with the responsibility that falls to those persons in a culture who have the power of prerogative. By prerogative we mean the ability and freedom to match resources with responsibility. In our American culture the white, the male, and the ruling generation has the prerogative. The non-white, the female, the very young and the very old often do not, and therefore they do not have access to resources to meet their own needs. The freedom and privilege to allocate resources, small or large, is most often the prerogative of ruling white males.

In a family, there is usually a dominant person whom most family members acknowledge as the leader. There is a scriptural term we believe perfectly captures this responsibility of leadership, or prerogative; it is *servanthood*, embodied in our Lord Jesus Christ. The Apostle Paul described Jesus as one who did not cling to the prerogatives of power, but instead laid aside his privileges to become a servant even to the point of ultimate sacrifice. Serving others is what empowerment is all about (cf. Phil. 2:5-8). Ours would be a different world indeed if the privileges of race, gender, and age were not hoarded self-protectively but rather distributed fairly and equitably. In sum, we believe that ideal fathering wants a free and just world and works actively to create that kind of environment in the family.

TRANSITIONAL GRACE

Because of the grace of God, Dennis has become a transitional person for his family in terms of the "birthmarks" issues he faced. He has learned to protect even though he himself often felt unprotected. He has learned to direct even though he was not directed. (We all agree he lacked somewhat in the area of discipline; that responsibility most often fell to Lucy.) And, he has learned to empower even though he was not empowered.

As we have dealt with the issues of the transitional person, we as a family have become powerfully aware of God's grace to us through His work in Dennis's life. God has been good to us in that he has been especially good to Dennis. For that, we all give Him thanks and praise.

CRUCIAL QUESTIONS

Based upon the focus of this chapter, ask yourself the following questions about your family as it is revealed in your genogram:

— Were the children in each family or household unit "fathered" as we have suggested? If they were, by whom? If they weren't, why not?
— What have been the long-range consequences of the patterns you have observed?
— What can you see that has been passed on from generation to generation? What is missing?
— As you continue to evaluate yourself, what "hole" have you discovered in yourself in the same way Dennis found the "hole" inside himself?

The courage to ask hard questions of yourself is what becoming a transitional person is all about. It requires learning to "father" yourself in the same way you have learned to "mother" yourself, as was discussed in the previous chapter.

7.

The "Three A's" of Generational Dysfunction

Had Jacob been challenged to look back through the generations of his family as we did in chapter 4, perhaps he could have better understood his predicament. Of course, the patriarchal authority of Isaac and Abraham probably would have precluded him from making some of the choices possible for us today.

Fortunately, we are under no such limitations. We have the freedom to look back through our own generations to see the "birthmarks" that are there, whether good or bad. That freedom is the legacy we have

because of Christ. He has freed us from the "unconditional filial loyalty" of the Old Testament patriarchal
Jewish family to a conditional loyalty based upon the
congruence of family patterns with scriptural principles.

Unconditional filial loyalty refers to an unques-
tioned obedience to the older generation by the
younger, especially when it involves obedience or loyalty to parents. Conditional loyalty involves respect
given to the older generation by the younger out of respect for Christ. It involves a sense of responsibility for
one's aging parents without a blind obedience to their
demands. Our ultimate loyalty is to Christ, not to the
past or to the present. His call upon our lives is the ultimate litmus test by which we analyze our relational
patterns. And, to the degree that our relational patterns
are not congruent with our understanding of scriptural
principles and with generally understood healthy
functioning, we are compelled by the love of Christ to
change, to be transitional people.

A problem we each face in looking at our family issues is that of *generational anxiety.* We agree with the noted
family therapist Edwin Friedman that 70 percent of all
dysfunctional patterns in a family system can be explained
in terms of generational issues.* We believe, likewise, that
much of what is constructive and healthy can be explained
generationally as well. Yet people often are paralyzed when
investigating their "birthmarks" and those of their families
because of what feels like an overwhelming generalized
anxiety and its attendant fear. This anxiety easily sabotages
our motivation to be transitional people. Instead, we retreat to known, comfortable patterns, even when we are

---

* See Edwin H. Friedman, *Generation to Generation: Family
Process in Church and Synagogue* (New York: Guilford Press,
1985).

aware that these patterns are not congruent with the way we believe we "ought to be." The wedge between what we believe (the "ought") and what we are is the real presence of generational anxiety.

"Generational anxiety" can be visualized as a large circle which contains two smaller circles. The two smaller circles represent the related issues of addictions and abuse.

THE FIRST "A" IS FOR ANXIETY

Generational anxiety is *the conscious or unconscious sense of dread that comes to dominate the world view of an individual, couple, or family.* If the dread is unconscious, it is quite often transmuted into other forms. In the same way that a genetic mutation changes the genetic code of a species for good or for ill, generational anxiety can be transformed generation by generation.

First, we'll look at four ways to analyze anxiety in a family; then we'll look at the most common ways anxiety is transmuted generationally in the family patterns that determine how anger is expressed, often leading to abuse, and in the presence of addictions.

Abuse is the displacement of anxiety in a family through the inappropriate expression of anger. Addiction is the anesthetizing or deadening of the anxiety. Either way, the bottom line is dysfunctional and painful.

Situational Anxiety

This type of anxiety is the most observable. It is specific and identifiable, involving situations in the life of a family at any particular point in time. For instance, families get anxious when someone loses his / her job, when a close family member dies, when there is a divorce, when a new member joins the family through marriage, birth, or adoption, or when there is a natural disaster or accident. Situational anxiety is normal and functional. It causes the family system to muster its resources to meet the challenges of life and death.

Unfortunately, we sometimes take the Apostle Paul's encouragement to "be anxious for nothing" to mean that our normal anxiety over these kinds of situations is not acceptable. We take his encouragement to be a kind of spiritual cheerleading, in much the same way a cheerleader yells for his or her team to "block that kick," "hold that line," etc.

Paul himself was anxious even to the point of depression (see 2 Cor. 7:5-7) and was pulled out of it by God's provision of a real-life comforter, his friend Titus. When Titus became Paul's cheerleader, his depression and anxiety passed. The cheerleader realizes that his / her encouragement is not an absolute but rather the expression of a preference. It's what you "wish" for the other.

In chapter 2 we discussed the story of one of Dennis's clients whose husband had stopped working and was letting his business slip into bankruptcy. His wife was appropriately, that is, situationally, anxious. His explanation for his attitude was that "Jesus would take care of everything." He claimed to trust God for new business and chose not to go out and solicit clients. His choices were more an escape from responsibility than a good faith effort to honor the commitment to his family, a commitment he made when he started the business. Rather than accept his anxiety for what it was, he became immobilized and rationalized his inaction as "trusting God." His attitude was more a caricature of Paul's teaching than a faithful and accurate interpretation.

Paul was not institutionalizing a passivity that leads to irresponsibility when he encouraged his readers to "be anxious for nothing." Instead, he was encouraging those who worry about everyday life to take the presence of Christ into account when they evaluate their situations and circumstances. Situational anxiety is normal, even helpful. It mobilizes resources. Normally, it passes when the reason for the anxiety passes.

Huddled Anxiety

Picture, if you will, an arctic scene where a herd of musk oxen are under attack by a pack of wolves. The horned, thick-coated oxen are gathered in a circle, facing outward, with their young protected in the center. The wolves prowl around the circle but can't penetrate the defenses of the herd. The young are protected. The wolves instinctively recognize their assault to be futile and they move on. The oxen are safe for another day.

Some families have that kind of "huddled" mentality even though the danger they face may be vague and unspecified. What they share with one another is a common, shared point of view: "It's us against them. It's safe in here. It's unsafe out there." The logical consequence of this fortress mentality is a suspicion about the outside world. The greater the suspicion, the higher the walls and the greater the anxiety.

We remember discussions we had with friends about whether to send our children to public or parochial schools. At stake were our spiritual values and our educational philosophy. We took this decision very seriously.

On one side of the debate were those parents whose suspicion of the influence of "secular humanism" on public schools caused them to encourage us to send our children to private schools. Additional concerns were the quality of education and issues of safety. On the other hand were the parents who viewed parochial schools as an escape from reality and enclaves of privilege.

We came to the conclusion that our commitment to freedom and liberty as an American ideal included public education. And our belief in Christ included confidence in our children and God's presence with them. We decided that our children would derive their values mostly from us and that they needed to face the realities and temptations of living as Christians in a sometimes difficult, even hostile, world. We were to be "salt" and "light." We've rarely regretted our decision although we respect parents who have come to different conclusions. We chose not to "huddle" in private schools.

Hidden Anxiety

Anxiety that is hidden involves an *unconscious dread usually related to the fear of abandonment or abuse.* The generational experience of one of Dennis's students provides a good illustration.

In doing his genogram, the student discovered that three generations before, a great-grandfather on his mother's side had abandoned his family, never to appear again. The great-grandmother had done the best she could, but she soon had a nervous breakdown and the responsibility for keeping the family together fell to the two eldest children, who were fifteen and sixteen at the time. The two teenagers had gotten work and were able to help the family get by. The fifteen-year-old, a son, joined the Navy at the outbreak of World War II when he was seventeen years old. Upon returning from the war, he married and settled down near his mother and younger brothers and sisters. He was Dennis's student's grandfather. The sixteen-year-old, a girl, never married and lived with her mother until the mother's death. She was now an independent but patronizing woman in her late seventies.

The hidden anxiety in the family was the powerful spoken and unspoken message about abandonment: "Never leave." Subsequently, all of the children and grandchildren had grown up, married, and lived within ten miles of the grandparents' home.

There were two exceptions. The first exception was one of the student's cousins who left the family circle to go to college, where she had met a young man of another faith, married him, and now lived in a distant city. This perceived "abandonment" of her family resulted in her being shunned by the family.

The second exception was Dennis's student. He had decided to leave the family farm and go to seminary in California in order to study for a career in the ministry. As the student shared his story with the class, he became aware of the powerful emotions he felt deep inside. He felt "tethered" to his family by his grandfather's fear of abandonment which had been passed down through the generations.

The student wanted the freedom to choose where he would serve God. But he loved his family and yearned for their support. He knew that wherever he chose to live, he would still communicate with and visit the family regularly. He wanted them to find a way to adapt their definition of family to include those members who lived beyond the ten-mile limit.

He decided that during his Christmas vacation he would talk with his grandfather and with his parents about his fears. He realized also that, in all probability, if he chose not to return to the family circle, he too would be shunned.

Christmas that year took on inordinate importance. When he returned to school the following January, the student reported mixed results. His parents had understood but his grandfather hadn't. After much thought, the student had decided that he would risk the grandfather's alienation and would choose to go wherever he felt "called." His parents were able to bless him in his decision, and they agreed to pray and hope for the grandfather's eventual acceptance and understanding. The student returned to school renewed. He had recognized his unhealthy "birthmark" (his hidden generational fear) and had taken a first step to correct it. He had begun the "transitional process."

Hurdled Anxiety

"Hurdled anxiety" is *anxiety that has been recognized for what it is and has been dealt with appropriately.* Like a hurdler on a track team, each individual must identify and cross the barriers he / she sees before him / her. This hurdled anxiety is the end product of the student's journey described above.

One word of caution, however. *Anxiety faced is not anxiety erased.* Because you have faced your generational anxiety once doesn't mean you'll not have to face it again. This is especially true of unconscious, hidden anxiety. In the case of the "tethered" student described above, the hidden anxiety of his grandfather will probably appear again when he has his own children and is asked to face the natural separation anxiety experienced by every parent. He will be faced with the temptation to hold on and to tether his young to him as did his grandfather. Hidden anxiety doesn't just go away when it has been hurdled. It will need to be hurdled again and again.

THE SECOND "A" IS FOR ABUSE

Anger is a legitimate human emotion that is stimulated by real and / or perceived threat or injury. When we get angry, it's usually for a reason. However, not all anger is tied to an immediate threat even though it may be provoked by an immediate stimulus. *Abuse is related to anger in that it is the illegitimate expression of anger toward another person characterized by violent actions or the threat of violence toward that person. As such, abuse involves physical, emotional, or sexual violence or the threat of violence toward one human being by another.* Recent years have seen a dramatic increase in abusive incidents, especially in families. Most of us have one or more friends who have been victims of abuse. Often, these "friends" may be in our own family. They may even be us.

While abusive incidents have been traditionally kept secret (that is, spouses, friends, and family members don't know or don't speak of them if they do know), more recently courtrooms, newsrooms, and classrooms seem to have the issues of abuse on full display. Interestingly, though, this is not the case in churches. We believe that prevention through education, confrontation, and litigation is very important and must be supported by the people of God, even though we don't yet agree on specific definitions, treatment plans (for abused or abuser), or even causes.

We suggest that all abuse results from anger which is inappropriately expressed as violence. And, to be transitional people, we must understand the generational patterns, the "birthmarks," which influence our own expression of the emotion, identify appropriate expressions of it, identify inappropriate/abusive patterns, and take necessary steps to prevent our own or other's abuse.

First, we will look at generational patterns that lead individually and culturally to abusive behaviors. Second, we will discuss a more functional alternative. Finally, we will present several suggestions for preventing abuse whether of others or ourselves.

The first generational pattern dealing with anger and abuse is that of aggression. Typically, aggressive behavior takes the form of hatred and bullying.

When we think about hatred, the blood feuds of the Middle East and South Africa and the sectarian violence of Northern Ireland come to mind. On a smaller scale, some patterns of hatred reach from generation to generation as racism and prejudice.

We recently viewed a Public Broadcasting Special on racial hatred in Brooklyn. We can still see the distorted and twisted faces of the white crowd as the blacks walked through the streets of Bensonhurst in New York City. The racism was equally distributed through the age groups that ringed the street. Old and young alike yelled epithets of threatened violence. The scene was ugly and unruly; the hatred was pervasive. Such patterns of hatred as racism, sexism, classism, etc., are typically generational in origin.

A second form of aggression in families is bullying.

A thirteen-year-old was referred by his school principal for counseling because of his violent outbursts in the classroom and his verbal abuse of teachers. When he sat in Dennis's office he was sullen and moody. His mother was nervous and worried. Within a few minutes of the beginning of the session, the boy screamed out, "I hate my father. I hate him. I hate him." The following story emerged.

Two nights before, the boy and his friend were watching professional basketball on television. It was a championship series involving the local team. Both boys were animated and excited. In the middle of the third quarter the boy's father noticed that his son had scratched an initial on his forearm.

"What's that?" the father inquired.

"It's nothing," replied the boy.

The father wouldn't let up, and the situation deteriorated into a verbal bashing of the boy by his father. When the yelling subsided, the father reached over and changed channels on the TV, turning off the basketball game. The boy asked him to turn the game back on. The father refused. He wanted to watch something else and that was that. The boy, humiliated by the exchange and his father's authoritarian behavior, stormed out of the room and into his bedroom, slamming the door behind him. The friend left, confused and embarrassed. The mother listened fearfully in the kitchen. When she tried to intervene, the father yelled at her to "shut up." She returned to her bedroom in tears. All three—the son, the friend, and the mother—felt bullied by the father. The incident at school involving a teacher followed two days later.

In the case of this family, the father had been abused as a boy by his older brothers, who picked on him mercilessly until he got too big and began to fight back. Bullying is typically a generational pattern involving dysfunctional expression of anger. It is always abusive.

A second generational pattern is an opposite way of expressing anger: abject passivity. In the case of the abused boy above, the mother was plagued by passivity. Her passivity, it turned out, took two forms—denial and victimization.

Although the father's abuse of the family had gone on for years, the mother had denied it to herself until her son's behavior at school deteriorated. When she heard her son scream that he hated his father, the truth struck home. She had pretended too long.

What she discovered in therapy was a pattern of feeling like a victim. She allowed herself and her children to be verbally "kicked around." In the same way abusers breed abusers, victims breed victims. The mother disclosed, as we talked, that her oldest child, a daughter, was in therapy because of a current physically abusive relationship. What for the most part was verbal abuse and bullying in the mother's generation had become full-blown physical abuse in the daughter's generation. The mother was embarrassed and overwhelmed when she made the connection. Changing the pattern of abuse would require her to stand up to her own fear of her husband and to break the standard of passivity (her "birthmark") she had learned in her own family of origin.

When she finally said, "No more!" she was energized and excited. She expected the worst and the worst hadn't happened. The father agreed to go to family counseling (although he later dropped out), and the mother was released from her fear. The years ahead will determine what the children will do with the patterns they have experienced in this home. It's now up to them.

The third generational pattern for expressing anger that often leads to abuse is that of the passive-aggressive person. Passive-aggressive people don't get angry. They get even. Patterns such as "scapegoating," in which an innocent victim is singled out for abuse rather than the person at whom the passive-aggressive is really mad, are common. Often in the case of incest and child abuse, the father or father substitute is angry at his wife but chooses to express his anger at her by abusing her child, frequently a daughter. The child becomes the casualty of a father's passive-aggressive behavior.

Another pattern is that of "stamp-saving" or "gunnysacking" one's anger. In this pattern the passive-aggressive person doesn't seem to get angry at the time of the offense. Instead, he / she stacks the anger inside like stacking wood for the fireplace. One day, when the stack is complete, he / she decides to burn it all at once. The person who is in the room at the time of the fire catches the heat for all of the previous unexpressed angry feelings.

The anger and subsequent abuse is disproportionate to the provoking incident. The one who is abused, of course, doesn't know this. He / she only experiences the wrath of the one who is angry, usually blaming him / herself for whatever is going on. The passive-aggressive pattern is confusing at best and hurtful, destructive, and abusive at worst.

The final generational pattern for handling anger is assertiveness. Assertive persons are able to distinguish between angry feelings and angry actions. When they feel anger, they are able to express it in a constructive way rather than a destructive one. Usually this takes the form of a simple declarative sentence: "I am angry because . . . ," or words to that effect. Second, they are able to select an appropriate time and an appropriate place to verbalize their feelings. They have their emotions sufficiently under control to be able to wait for another time or place to express them. They use that time to clarify their feelings rather than to diffuse them. Third, they are able to clarify and directly express their feelings and the hurt behind them. They understand that they get angry for a reason. Most often the reason is one of hurt. They find a way to identify the pain beneath their anger, sometimes through reflection and other times through the input of a trusted confidant, such as a counselor or therapist. The assertive person takes initiative and seeks consultation with others as needed.

Steps to Prevent Abusive Behavior

Abusive behavior, or its threat, destroys families. It betrays trust and fosters fear, anxiety, and even complete withdrawal from everyday functioning. A program of prevention dealing with the issue of abuse in families involves steps that move from the specific to the general, from the individual to the society.

1. Accept as fact that abuse is always wrong. It is never right to initiate violence toward another human being or to threaten a person with violence. The social implications of such a position warrant extensive discussion. Put the issue on top of the table and talk about it.

2. Recognize that abuse is defined by the victim's perception of it rather than the attitude of the one who is the actor. That is, you can abuse someone even though you don't intend to do so. We must always ask ourselves how the other person is experiencing or perceiving our actions. Their reality is important.

3. Recognize that abuse is a generational issue. Abusers beget abusers and victims beget victims. Deliberate and intentional choices must be made in order to stop the generational patterns.

4. If abuse is suspected, act as if it is true. That is, if you're going to err, err on the side of action rather than caution. Often, simply doing something is enough to deter the abuse. Don't get caught in the position of victimizing the victim. Likewise, be open to the possibility that abuse may not have occurred. Objectivity is the key.

5. If you have been abused or have been an abuser, seek professional help. Don't treat the issue as if it's past and forgotten. Deal actively with the matter as you would with a serious medical problem such as suspected cancer or heart disease.

6. Recognize that anyone can be an abuser or a victim. If someone you know appears to be abused, talk to her/him about it. If someone you know appears to be abusing someone else, confront him/her about it, taking a witness with you when you do. Don't participate in the conspiracy of silence about the issue.

7. When you know there is abuse or have a strong suspicion about it, gather as a community (that is, join

with others who care about the person) and do something about it. Draw a figurative line in the sand and say to the abuser that the community (as defined above) will not tolerate the continued abuse. Surround the victim with your support. Protect the privacy and dignity of both the victim and the abuser and avoid stigmatizing either whenever possible.

8. Be ready as a community to shield the victim from the abuser, either through distance or through the creation of protective barriers such as a home for abused women and their children might provide.

9. Clearly, pro-actively, and in public, state the position of the community regarding abuse. Go on record against the behavior. Stand with victims and against abusers. Support legislation against abuse. Treat abuse as sin.

10. Actively engage in programs of responsible reconciliation in which the burden of proof is upon the abuser to demonstrate changed behavior rather than upon the victim. Be open to the fact that abusers can be healed, but don't be seduced into easy and cheap repentance. Make sure the way of restoration is known to the abuser.

THE THIRD "A" IS FOR ADDICTION

Addiction is the physical or psychological domination by a substance or situation that is able to exert undue influence over the behavior and prevailing attitude of the person. Addictive behaviors are used to numb or anesthetize the pain of anxiety.

While our intention is to identify situations or substances that exert undue influence, we hope to focus on ways for transitional people to seek moderation and self-control in their lives rather than domination. The list that follows is by no means exhaustive. We have selected these addictions, moving from the obvious to the more subtle, because in our experience they seem to influence the American family the most.

The most pervasive addiction in our culture today is that of substance and chemical abuse. Alcoholism and drug addiction are rampant in our society — in our churches, families, schools, work places, and elsewhere. The devastation caused by that abuse is well documented.

Our addition to the discussion is to relate addictive behavior to generational anxiety rather than relate it totally to irresponsibility on the part of the addicted person. Our observation in the scores of genograms that we have evaluated is that whenever there is a problem of substance abuse in a particular generation, usually there is a precipitating cause or dysfunction upstream in the family. In the context of this book, we can call it a "birthmark." The substance abuse is simultaneously an effect and a cause. It is the result of what has gone before and it is the cause of what happens after. The addiction of substance abuse is particularly hurtful and damaging.

The second prevailing addiction is that of food. Although the abuse of food in our culture is not as notorious as substance abuse, the consequences are probably as chronic. The fad diets that sell books by the millions play upon the individual's need to get a quick fix over the anxiety of the past.

Take, for example, the case of a young woman we know of who is more than a hundred pounds overweight. Only recently, through therapy, was she able to acknowledge to herself that she was the victim of sexual abuse by her father at a very early age. All through her past, she had used food in two ways.

First of all, she uses food to give herself comfort when she becomes fearful or agitated. She now remembers that as a child when she would cry — and she had reason to — her mother would give her something to eat to quiet her down. As an adult, she is carrying on the pattern.

Second, she uses the weight that was a direct consequence of her overeating to make herself sexually unattractive to men so as not to need to face the anxiety of her own sexually conflicted impulses. Food has become a comfort and a shield.

Part of our contemporary culture is the media hype that tells us that eating and drinking bring pleasure. Self-control doesn't, they imply.

In the media, especially television, the irony is that the person who is eating and / or drinking the product being sold is usually thin and may well be exercising. Never do you see the consumer in his or her naturally obese state. That doesn't sell doughnuts. Food is the most ubiquitous addiction today.

The third addiction is sex. Sex is used for everything today. It sells cars, beer, perfume, and everything else under the sun. It sells books, films, cable television, and videos. What we have become is a society that believes sex is the ultimate anxiety reducer. Having an orgasm will make the pain go away.

Again, the irony is that pursuing sexual orgasm as a solution to one's anxiety causes the escalation of sexual stimulation. Although an orgasm may temporarily reduce the tension associated with anxiety, the desire for it will only build higher the next time. Ultimately, like any addictive behavior, the anxiety becomes greater than the ability of the substance to satisfy it. The addict is caught in a destructive loop leading to ever more hurtful patterns, which in turn generate additional anxiety.

The fourth addiction is work. The need is to be productive in order to feel good about oneself. Work in and of itself is not addictive. Only when it is used to protect oneself from feeling unimportant or to insulate oneself from the demands of significant relationships does it become addictive. There may be benefits attached to work addiction, but with respect to the family, the workaholic is like an absentee landlord. His influence is felt though his literal presence isn't. It would be better for all concerned if he were physically and emotionally available.

Associated with the addiction of work, but separate from it, is the addiction to success. Ours is a society of winners that is intolerant of losers. Bigger is better. More is good.

The example we are most familiar with is the ministry as a career. For example, most seminaries have a pastor-in-residence program. The goals of such a program are to bring ministers to campus to give students the opportunity to interact with them about the pragmatics of ministry. However, most of the pastors who are invited are the pastors of the largest and most successful churches — this in spite of the fact that the average graduate will serve in a church of less than 200 members and will suffer several experiences of frustration and failure along the way. Without meaning to, seminaries have bought into the success motif and are sending the message to the graduate that if he or she is average (that is, in a church of less than 200) he / she will not be thought of as successful.

What is true of pastor-in-residence programs is true of the ministry in general. Does a pastor ever feel "called by God" to move from a large church to a smaller one? It may happen, but it is the exception to the rule. Some clergy, like some of us, are addicted to success and to winning.

A recent item in the *Los Angeles Times* illustrates the same problem in terms of parent-child relationships.* In an article entitled "Fast-Track Childhoods" the parenting styles of successful, high-achieving, dual-career parents were discussed. What caught our eye was the emphasis of these parents upon the end product (winning the trophy, getting the top grade, i.e., "success") rather than upon the process (playing the game, trying hard, etc.). The writer ends the piece with an especially relevant quote from the headmaster of a high-powered prep school in the Los Angeles area, someone who lives with the problem daily:

> Success, without anything holding it up, is a pretty empty goal. Separated from a value system that sees an individual in relation to the cosmos, it is meaningless. Kids who see their parents willing to sacrifice everything in order to succeed are sure to ask, "Is that all there is?"

Those of us who become addicted to success are like Garrison Keillor's inhabitants of Lake Woebegon, where "all the children are above average." We need to remember that our children take their value systems from us. Rather than focusing upon their successes, we need to empower them to live meaningful and productive lives. It is to be hoped that the influence of our value system upon them will have something to do with how they come to define meaning and productivity.

* "Fast-Track Childhoods" by Bettijane Levine, *Los Angeles Times*, September 2, 1990.

Last in our discussion of addictions is the cultural addiction to material goods. Things matter. There is a bumper sticker that reads, "He who has the most toys wins." That is more true than we would like to admit. Materialism is a subtle mistress who seduces us into believing that happiness comes from being comfortable, from being surrounded with tangible objects. Jesus said, "What shall it profit a man, if he shall gain the whole world, and lose his own soul?" (Mark 8:36, KJV). He was talking to his disciples about this addiction.

Think through your last week. How much of it was taken up with the pursuit, acquisition, or maintenance of material goods? The addiction to things, in which they come to own us rather than we them, is a disease of the twentieth-century middle class. Moving up means having more. The higher you get, the more you have. Bigger is better. More is good.

If it appears that we are advocating a life of spartan denial, let us assure you we're not. Rather, we're advocating a position of moderation, not domination. This involves a decision as to how much is enough, and it's better to make that choice before the fact than after. Making the decision after the fact is the reason our credit cards get so out of line and our bills creep up to consume our income. Moderation is an issue of lifestyle and of human choice. As transitional people, we must make the decision.

TOUGH QUESTIONS

Anxiety, abuse, and addiction are the "triple A's" of generational patterns. As you look at your genogram, think in terms of yourself. Use the genogram as a mirror. Let it show you what dominates your life. When you have looked at yourself hard in that mirror, next let your genogram answer the question of where you might have picked up the "birthmarks" (generational patterns) that you have identified. Only after you have looked at yourself objectively can you look with integrity at the others around and before you.

The Nelsons are an example of a family that faced the tough questions and came away from the experience as changed people.

They came to our attention through the weekend indiscretion of one of their adolescent sons. He had borrowed the family car, supposedly to go to a church which had gospel rock concerts on Saturday evenings. Instead, he and his friends had gone to the Los Angeles Convention Center to hear a Pink Floyd concert. At the concert one of the boys in the car was arrested by the police for marijuana possession. In the scuffle surrounding his arrest, the Nelsons' son had been arrested as well. At 1:00 A.M. the parents drove the forty plus miles to downtown Los Angeles to bail their eighteen-year-old son out of jail. When they picked him up they were angry and frightened. He was defensive and resentful. The drive home was a stand-off.

In the ensuing weeks, the parents came to realize that they had created a paradoxical situation. Their overprotectiveness had led to their children's heightened curiosity and interest in the unknown. By shutting them up in a closed world, they had actually created a fascination with what was outside the "huddle."

When we met with them as a family and pushed the issues deeper, two enlightening incidents in the parents' teenage years came to light.

As an adolescent, the father had been in an automobile accident in which he and his friends were seriously injured. They had been drinking at the time. He had never rid himself of the memories of the accident.

The mother shared an equally distressing experience. When she was fifteen she had gone to a party where she had become drunk. Evidently she had sex with the boy who took her to the party, and she became pregnant. When her mother and father found out about the pregnancy, they insisted she have an abortion (illegal at the time). She had the abortion and went on with her life, marrying her husband when she was in her early twenties. Together they "huddled" and began their family.

In family therapy the parents decided to share these secrets with their children, the result was a dramatic releasing of their anxiety.

The children were able to comfort their parents as their emotions regarding the past burst to the surface. In the weeks of healing that followed the parents were able to "let their children go." They decided to trust them to make their own choices and, hopefully, not to make the kind of mistakes that had shadowed them all of their adult lives. Or, if mistakes did occur, they would work together to handle them as transparently and as maturely as possible. Their fortress mentality had not worked, and their anxiety had turned out to be worse than the consequences they feared. Their sharing of the information about their past was a *transitional moment* for their family.

8.

Come Close, Go Away

The first year of marriage is the hardest for many married couples. What makes it difficult is a complex question to answer, but probably among its most challenging issues is the matter of closeness and distance. This issue is one that bothers most families throughout their history as they attempt to learn just how much togetherness and how much separateness their relationship will tolerate. Discovering what is comfortable in terms of closeness and distance is relevant not only for couples, but for parent / child and sibling relationships.

For example, when Dennis and Lucy married they came into the relationship with different expectations regarding levels of togetherness and separateness.

Lucy, the eldest of six children, is from a family in which most members prefer a high level of interaction or closeness. Her mother, in particular, likes and encourages togetherness for the family. It's almost as if the family isn't "together" unless everyone is present. Family gatherings are held regularly. Family members alternate taking the initiative for getting together even though the times of togetherness can be fairly intense, and include occasional conflict. The reason for getting together is a collective desire. Letters are written, but less frequently than gathering occurs. Privacy and solitude are sometimes difficult to find. It's as if the forever-open doors between the rooms of Lucy's childhood home have carried over symbolically into the relationships between family members.

In contrast, Dennis was raised as an only child of a single parent. Even though his extended family lived nearby, the interaction between them, even at family gatherings, was sparse, that is, distant. Historically, their desire for getting together involved his grandmother. When the family gathered for holidays or special occasions, it was at her request. When she died the family stopped gathering together as a whole except for an infrequent wedding or funeral.

When Lucy's family got together on holidays, they typically played cards, usually pinochle. There were as many tables as were needed for the number in attendance. In this family, one of the marks of being accepted as "nearly grownup" was being invited to play cards at family gatherings. The games were competitive, often boisterous. Laughing, whooping, hollering, and sometimes verbalized anger were the rule of the day. The game was the family's metaphor of togetherness. Those who chose not to play cards were made to feel uncomfortable, not quite "part of the family group." When the family came together, the in-laws were pressured to "fit in." If they chose not to, they were marginalized and excluded in the subtlest of ways.

When Dennis's family got together on holidays, the men tended to retreat outside to the garage, where they talked. The women stayed inside and visited. If the genders did mix, they sat in the living room and passively watched television, usually a sports program. Nothing much was said, even though everyone was in the room. There was little interaction. The separation of the sexes and the passive watching of TV were the metaphors of the family's separateness.

Women and men had little to interact about together. When the family gathered, the "togetherness" took the form of observation. Members were never quite sure how others felt or what they thought. In-laws, as a result, were uncertain how to relate and were uncomfortable as to whether or not they were considered part of the "family."

As you can see, the "birthmarks" we inherited from our two families looked markedly different. It is not surprising that during our first year of marriage, these differences between us began to show.

Lucy turned her energy to making our apartment into a home. After work, she planned our evening meals with care and energy. Being married meant being "together" — for meals, for shopping, for talking, for recreation; asleep, awake, all of the time.

Dennis, on the other hand, liked the idea of togetherness but needed his distance. So he went to school full time to finish his undergraduate degree, worked part time, and volunteered as the youth director in a struggling church. The time left for togetherness, which included, hopefully, good sex and an occasional football game on TV, was limited.

The pattern of the first year was a metaphor of the next several years of our relationship — Lucy wanting, even needing, more togetherness and Dennis wanting, yes, needing, more separateness. The arguments increased as we each made seemingly incompatible demands on one another.

Through the years our individual needs for togetherness and separateness have ebbed and flowed. Each of us has seen our wants and our needs change. After thirty years of marriage we have learned that in our family "the urge to merge" — the need for togetherness and closeness — and "the need to leave" — the need for separateness and distance — exist simultaneously, usually in tension with one another. Learning to manage the tension is what accounts in large measure for family health. Failing to manage the tension is what accounts for much family dysfunction.

Our understanding of family dynamics as related to closeness and distance is summarized by three words, each describing an emotional mechanism or pattern the persons in a family adopt for themselves as a way of coping with the closeness / distance tension. The three patterns are (1) disengagement, (2) fusion, and (3) differentiation. Each pattern or mechanism for coping with the issues of closeness and distance will be discussed in terms of three family agendas: the need to attach or bond, the need to establish boundaries, and the need to have choices. Attachment, boundaries, and choice can easily be remembered as the "ABCs" of family togetherness and separation.

As we discuss each coping mechanism, ask yourself if that pattern seems to fit you. Next, ask yourself if the pattern fits anyone else in your family. Last of all, ask the same question of your family's generations. Are there any consistent themes that run from generation to generation? If there are, what have been the consequences of those themes or "birthmarks"?

DISENGAGEMENT

Persons who use disengagement as their pattern for managing togetherness and separateness are using distance both physically and emotionally to feel comfortable and to gain the separateness they need. Physically, attaining separation may take the form of running away from home, walking out of the room and slamming the door during an argument, or some similar action. Often, even in the smallest of interactions, persons who are disengaged, because of the emotions involved, find it difficult to look another person in the eye when they're conversing, particularly if the conversation is about them. Disengaged persons have learned to manage the intensity of their emotions by creating distance between themselves and others.

Now, let's look at the "ABCs" of disengagement.

Attachment

Persons who have too little attachment, too much distance, are like "loose balloons." They rise above their relationships and break away with little thought of how their actions affect those who are left behind. "Loose balloons" have the memory and, perhaps, the appearance of being attached. The reality is that their behaviors are characterized by the need for freedom more than by the need for connectedness.

A dramatic example of the "loose balloon" phenomenon can be found in the New Testament story of the prodigal son. His need for distance from his father and his brother "drove him into a far country" where he became miserable and defeated.

To a lesser degree, a "loose balloon" example exists in our own home. Dennis tends to fit into this category. Only recently, through his own therapy, Dennis was able to recognize that some of his motives for seeking graduate degrees (he has three of them) and ministry were mixed. Ministry for Dennis has included regularly leaving home and speaking in faraway places and countries. When he was in school or traveling, his motives were contained in a package adorned with a benign ribbon called "serving God." That there were two ribbons was never recognized. The overt motive or ribbon was called "ministry" and the covert one was called "the need for distance."

He frequently wanted to be away, to have time alone, but his stated explanations to Lucy were different. She often felt frustrated. She wanted him to serve God as he wished, but she also wanted a greater sense of connectedness with him. It can be tough to live with someone whose "birthmark" is a "loose balloon," especially if the need for closeness or distance varies significantly between partners. It is easy for the "loose balloon" kind of person to mask the need for freedom with other apparently benevolent motives. "I need to be alone" becomes "I need to pray." "I need to feel free" becomes "I am off to serve God." If you're the partner who needs more closeness, you're in a double-bind. You want your spouse to serve God as he is called, but, according to his rules, serving God necessitates his going away. You also want the closeness that comes from being with him, but his needs, wrapped in God-words, get in the way. It would be much better for both partners to acknowledge, frankly and honestly, what the issues really are and to proceed from there.

Boundaries

Like attachment, boundaries relate to spatial or physical issues as well as emotional comfort. Disengaged persons seem to others to be living behind a sign saying "No trespassing! This means you!" Spatially, they create distance by setting up barricades between themselves and others—closed doors, stereo headphones, separate bedrooms, etc. Their emotional doors seem to be locked and bolted. Though physically present, they send signals to others which say, "Do not enter," "Do not disturb," or "For emergency only."

A pastor we knew sent those kinds of confusing messages to his congregation. At the door on Sundays following the morning service, in his role of pastor, he seemed to invite personal contact and relationship. However, during the week he was inaccessible to his people and distant. He ventured out of his home or office only for a politically select few and then only in the case of an emergency. The congregation was consistently confused and disappointed. His "birthmark" was the need to be disengaged, but he couldn't own it.

A disengaged person, consciously or unconsciously, imposes boundaries so rigid and impenetrable that you have no hope of making contact, no matter how desperate your need. You are left feeling that the "loose balloon" doesn't care about you even if he / she says he / she does.

Choice

The third agenda affecting closeness and distance involves making choices. Are choices left open to you or are they made for you?

Disengaged persons' decisions tend to be "fixed," carved in stone. When they have made up their minds, it's over. The discussion is closed;. the issue is settled. It's the Archie Bunker syndrome — once he had his mind made up, no one could change it even if he must have known he was clearly wrong.

Suppose, for example, that a disengaged person decides that he is never going to see you or have anything to do with you because you have done or said something to hurt him. This person will probably not be responsive to requests to discuss the situation and may not even accept an apology should you offer one. He may even decide to behave as if nothing is wrong and everything is the way it always has been. Usually, no explanations or discussions for his attitudes and actions are offered; his decisions, once made, are simply announced, with the assumption that they will be followed by all concerned. Since there is little (or no) opportunity for dialog and negotiation, this rigidity can be frustrating for his loved ones. It makes little difference that the partner of the disengaged person may choose to "do the right thing" or that she / he is deciding as she / he does because she / he loves her / his spouse or family very much. The disengaged person hasn't understood, or even heard, the other person's point of view. Typically, others haven't been able to express their thoughts or feelings about the issue. Their choices have been limited arbitrarily.

Understandably, then, disengaged people tend to feel lonely and isolated. They are prone to depression and feelings of detachment. They don't let others in and it's tough for them to get out. They live with a fear and dread of rejection.

FUSION

At the other end of the continuum from the disengaged person is the person who "fuses" with another individual. This unhealthy relationship results from the failure of an individual to develop a strong enough identity to function independently. Instead, such a person fuses with those around him or her and functions as if he / she had actually become that other person. His / her emotional survival, at least unconsciously, depends upon the survival of the other, almost as totally as a fetus's physical survival depends upon its mother's well-being.

Fusion may also be described as "enmeshment." Fusion connotes the blurring of boundaries. In the context of this chapter, enmeshment connotes the tangling up of personal identities. Enmeshment is easy to visualize as being like a fishing line that has become so snarled that it can't be rewound but must be cut off before starting over again.

Attachment

In terms of bonding, the person who fuses with others suffers from too much attachment, or connectedness.

It's impossible to discern where one person ends and the other person begins.

A metaphor we use to help counselees visualize the tenacity of this kind of bonding is "super-glue." According to the commercials touting this product, once two elements have been joined together with it, it's as if they are permanently bonded to one another; in fact, the line between the two is molecularly changed.

A person who fuses with another reaches out, grabs, and holds onto that person for dear life. Those who have been glued to such a person feel stifled and smothered in the process.

We remember, for example, a child who was plagued with school phobia. In the seventh grade she developed severe stomach cramps whenever she tried to go to school. It turned out that the fusion in her family's dynamics involved a mother whose marriage was terribly unhappy. She and her husband would have divorced had it not been for their religious convictions. Thus, though married, they lived as divorced people. The mother, who devoted herself to her children, unconsciously sent them the message "You can't live without me"; in fact, the message was "I will have nothing to live for without you." The school-phobic daughter, at the age when children begin to think about independence, instinctively decided that she would rescue her mother from her feelings of abandonment. She got sick and stayed sick, forcing the mother to stay home and care for her. The marriage remained intact because it focused on the illness of the child. The parents' solution, though dysfunctional, had been to home-school the daughter through the seventh grade. The "super-glue" made it unthinkable for the daughter to leave home to attend school with her peers.

Ultimately, the parents were unable to work through the issues in their marriage, and they divorced. Against her will, the mother reentered the work force, which fortunately led to her becoming a more autonomous person. The daughter too benefited from her parents' divorce as she subsequently returned to school and began to exercise her own autonomy. The school phobia lessened as the fusion diminished.

Boundaries

Persons who fuse with those around them live with the assumption that nothing's secret, nothing's private. This kind of person can be the parent who thinks nothing of walking into her / his teenager's room and rooting through dresser drawers. When she / he finds something she / he doesn't like, she / he takes the discovery as justification for violating the adolescent's spatial boundaries.

Some boundaries are physical or spatial, like those surrounding a woman on a subway or bus who normally doesn't expect her physical person to be violated by a wandering hand or arm of a man or woman standing next to her. Every person has the right to decide for her / himself what happens to her / his own body.

Other boundaries are temporal, like those that are violated when a person engages you in conversation without asking whether he / she is being intrusive or invasive and without considering you, your schedule, or your frame of mind.

Whatever the type of boundary — physical / spatial or temporal / emotional — the person who fuses (or enmeshes) with others is the person who typically acts as if boundaries don't exist. If such persons do recognize boundaries, they are the ones who decide what and where the boundaries begin and end. Nothing's appropriately secret or private.

Choice

The third characteristic of the fused person who has too much attachment and too little respect for the boundaries of others is the person who treats choices, either his / hers or the choices of those with whom they are fused, as a "rubber stamp."

A mother who was fused with her daughter, sat in Dennis's office with her daughter, saying, "There's no question at all. My daughter doesn't want to marry the boy, and that's that." In reality, her daughter was deeply in love with the young man and wanted very much to marry him. Her mother would hear nothing of it. What she wanted was for the daughter to agree with her perception of the situation. In fact, there was to be no argument about it. The daughter was expected to "rubber stamp" the mother's wishes.

Later, when the daughter asserted her independence and insisted that the choice to marry was hers, her mother threw a fit. She refused to attend the wedding, and she even wrote the daughter out of her will. "It's as if she's dead to me" was the mother's response.

Unfortunately for this family, the fusion between the mother and the daughter couldn't be broken without creating a complete breech in their relationship. The mother couldn't fathom that her daughter would make a decision and exercise her choice in such a way as to disagree with her.

A rubber stamp of an opposite kind is the person who finds her / himself constantly giving in to the decisions of others as if she / he has no choice of her / his own. A woman who, in deference to her husband's life and career, gives up her identity, has no interests of her own, and makes no decisions for herself, has ceased to be a person in her own right and has become a rubber stamp.

We are not talking, however, about all women who choose being a wife and a homemaker as their primary career. All homemakers are not rubber stamps. Take the case of Barbara Bush, the wife of President George Bush. The controversy surrounding her commencement address at an exclusive women's college on the East Coast is illustrative of the issues. When Mrs. Bush was announced as the commencement speaker, some of the graduating seniors objected, stating that she represented all that they had been encouraged not to become. They had been counseled to seek their place in the world of business, government, and education and to place family relationships lower in their priorities.

Mrs. Bush gave the commencement address, and she held to her position that her choice to be a wife and mother did not make her a second-class citizen. In fact, she encouraged the young women graduates not to neglect their significant relationships as they pursued their careers. She was and is not a rubber stamp.

The issue is not about whether a person is working inside or outside the home, whether he or she is male or female, etc.; it is about choice. Do family members have the capacity and the option to develop their own preferences? Can they express what they want and don't want? What they need and don't need? What they expect from one another? Does the family, or relationship, give respect to each person's perspective or interests?

We agree with Mrs. Bush. The issue is the issue of choice, of having the right to choose for oneself as a free and responsible person in one's own right.

DIFFERENTIATION

The third option in the matter of togetherness and separateness, closeness and distance, is the pattern of differentiation. This is a formal term from Family Systems literature meaning the ability of a person to hold the need for closeness and the need for distance in a state of healthy tension or balance. It involves the ability to remain a "different" person while simultaneously staying connected to those you love and care about.

Attachment

The differentiated person is someone who is able to bond without binding. The best metaphor we can think of is an amazing invention of the 1980s, the "Post-it," which allows us to paper our offices, refrigerators, and bulletin boards with notes to ourselves without the problem of residue when the note is removed. The note sticks. It bonds, yet releases, then bonds again as needed.

So it is with differentiated persons. Their bonding is clear and a connection is made. Relationships "stick" people together. However, when it comes time for one or the other to leave, for whatever reason, the relationship has the capacity to release the participants without giving up the ability to bond or stick, again when and where it is appropriate.

Differentiated persons neither disengage nor fuse in the face of relational demands. They are able to bond with and to release those whom they love. They are able to bless and celebrate their going. That blessing makes it possible for the one who leaves to return again without fear of being bound or swallowed up. The differentiated person's pattern of attachment has a curious sense of freedom associated with it.

Boundaries

Differentiated persons are also able to set limits. They know how to draw a line where they end and another person begins. If there were a sign on their bedroom door it would read, "Knock before entering." They grant access but demand respect. They give respect, as evidenced by their living by the rules they demand for themselves.

We were once in a group discussion about parent / teenager communication in which one of the parents asked what they should do if they walked in on their adolescent son while he was masturbating. One of the mothers immediately responded as a differentiated person when she said, "I would say 'excuse me' and close the door. In fact, the situation probably wouldn't happen because I would knock before I entered. The predicament just would not occur." Her answer has stuck with us ever since. "Knock before entering" says that you have the right to determine where and what your physical, emotional, temporal, and spatial boundaries are. Others have the responsibility to respect you and your limits.

Choice

The idea of choice in the context of differentiation is twofold: first, it means taking responsibility for your own self and the choices you make. Second, it means insisting that ultimately you are only responsible for what you have the power to control or influence. If you are being held responsible for something or someone you cannot control or if you are holding yourself responsible for that something or someone, you are probably not differentiated. Differentiated persons are comfortable knowing that they and others as well reap whatever they sow. They are able to make the difficult decision to let natural consequences take their course.

Of course, young children don't take care of themselves in terms of food, shelter, and other physical needs. On the other hand, you can expect an eighteen-year-old to be responsible for his or her own daily life, whether that involves washing his / her own clothes, cleaning his / her own room, managing his / her own money, and so on. Responsibility increases with age and maturity.

Likewise, differentiated persons find a way to understand and accept whatever is their reasonable responsibility for aging, disabled, or disadvantaged loved ones. The exception doesn't change the basic rule.

Becoming a differentiated person involves gradually assuming the responsibilities of adulthood simultaneously with being granted the privileges of being an adult. A differentiated person understands that freedom with responsibility is not the freedom to "do your own thing." It does involve the choice to assume a fair share of the responsibility that belongs to your family and community as a "bill-paying" adult. You bear the weight of the community proportionate to your ability to bear that weight. Becoming a responsible person involves accepting the principle that freedom has responsibility attached to it.

CONCLUSION

Disengagement, fusion, and differentiation — these are three patterns for handling the issues of closeness and distance in a relationship. Your family falls somewhere on the continuum between fusion at one end and disengagement on the other, probably not as neatly as we have suggested, but somewhere on the continuum in general.

Where would you place yourself on that continuum? How do you manage the issues of attachment, boundaries, and choice — the "ABCs" of togetherness and separateness? How successful are you at maintaining the balance or tension between the two?

What about the people with whom you are living? Where do they fall? Think back through some of the arguments or conflicts of the past year. Can those conflicts now be understood in a togetherness / separateness framework? If yes, which of the three major patterns (disengagement, fusion, and differentiation) characterizes the outcome of the conflict? If you could change anything about what happened, what would you have done differently?

If you have done a genogram, look at it now and ask of your generational family the same questions you have asked of yourself and the people with whom you are living in the present. Who were the disengagers, the fusers, the differentiated ones? What were the effects of their pattern upon your generational family? If something needs to change, what can you do to begin the process?

That's the role of the transitional person.

9.

The Paradox of Power

Newborn human infants are among the most helpless, dependent, and vulnerable of all living creatures. Yet their very helplessness is what gives them power over their caretakers. What mother or father with a new baby at home would deny that the very presence of the infant demands that they — mostly the mother — completely rearrange their lives? Regular sleep patterns are thrown out the window. Fatigue and financial insecurity are among the dominant worries reported in the research literature of families with new babies. The natural helplessness of the infant dominates the family. The infant has power over the parents, who are totally responsible for their child's survival.

Now, suppose it's seventeen years later. The infant has grown into a senior in high school. She is failing her classes. She is surly, moody, and defensive. The house is filled with pitched battles between her and her parents over her choice of friends. They fear she is using drugs.

Finally the whole spectacle explodes when she and her friends are arrested by the police for marijuana possession. The parents consult their pastor, and he refers them to a local drug treatment program. The professional staff at the hospital, after interviewing the girl, recommends hospitalization over a six-week period.

But there's a problem. The parents' medical insurance will pay for only 50 percent of the costs. The remaining 50 percent, probably in the neighborhood of $20,000, must be paid by the family. Finally, the decision is made. The parents refinance their home. The girl is hospitalized and the parents join the daughter in treatment. Business trips are rescheduled. Vacations are canceled. Hours are spent commuting to and from the hospital as the program's therapists attempt to bring healing to the family.

In her group therapy sessions in the hospital, ironically, the daughter rails on and on against her parents. She feels like a victim. Her mother is smothering and controlling. Her father is distant and neglectful. She feels angry and powerless.

When the same information surfaces during family therapy, the parents are flabbergasted. If they're so powerful, why do they feel so helpless? Why is their whole world being dominated by their drug-infected daughter? They are experiencing the same feelings of responsibility and subordination they felt when they first brought their infant daughter home from the hospital seventeen years earlier.

The illustration reflects *the paradox of power*. Often, the one who appears to have control doesn't, and the one who appears to be helpless is actually in control. Power isn't necessarily a function of status, gender, strength, size, intelligence, or maturity. Rather, *power is the ability to control the resources available to a family, community, or even a nation, by whatever means.* Despite her protests of being smothered and controlled, the daughter in this family had seized power because she and her addictions had taken control over the resources of her family.

A DEFINITION OF POWER

In the context of family relationships, there are three levels of power, based upon the answers to the following questions: (1) who does what? (2) who decides who does what? and (3) who decides the rules for determining numbers one and two?*

In the case of a newborn infant, power is a function of its helplessness—a reflection of levels two and three. The parents are often preempted from decisions because of the not-so-silent ability of the baby to let her demands be known. And the conventions of society regarding our responsibilities for child care (that is, the

---

* We borrow heavily in this section from the works of Jay Haley. In particular see J. Haley (ed.), *Changing Families* (New York: Grune & Stratton, 1971); *Uncommon Therapy* (New York: W. W. Norton, 1973); and *Leaving Home: The Therapy of Disturbed Young People* (New York: McGraw-Hill, 1980).

rules of parenting) give the infant the unspoken right to decide how we will decide.

In the case of the rebellious adolescent, her power was a function of her dependency and irresponsibility, both conditions fostered by her supposedly "powerful" parents. Such a notion of power allows a slightly different perspective when looking at the use and abuse of power in a family. Power rests in the hands of the person or persons in a system who individually or in concert with others controls the resources available to the members of the system.

A FAMILY'S RESOURCES

The second component in a definition of power has to do with whoever controls the "resources" in the family.* The resources we are referring to can be summarized in three categories: energy, space, and time.

"Energy" in a family is what a family *does*: its actions, activities, behaviors, etc. "Space" is *where* a family does what it does, the physical space inside the home and outside in the world. "Time" is *when*, during the twenty-four hours of the day and the twelve months of the year, a family does what it does.

The resources of a family have to do with a three-dimensional whole: involving the what, where and when of family interaction with one another and with their environment. Whoever controls the what, when, and where, effectively controls the family. That person (or persons) has (have) the power.

---

* Our definition of resources as well as much of the following discussion is taken from the writings of David Kantor and William Lehr, *Inside the Family* (San Francisco: Jossey-Bass, 1975).

THE POWER OF "WHAT"

Think about your genogram and the generations of your family in terms of power as we've defined it. Growing up as a child in your family, who did what? That is, who controlled the energy in your family?

Take, for example, the family chores.

Who washed the dishes? Who cooked the food? Who mowed the lawn? Who serviced the cars? Most families tend to sort these kinds of chores according to male and female roles. The women do one thing and the men do another. It's supposed to work out fairly with the work distributed evenly among the family members.

Years ago our family had to work through some of the issues regarding family power in terms of "what" it is that we do.

The issues came to a head one Sunday at the dinner table. Lucy was especially angry that she was being required to do most of the work for the household in addition to her full-time job.

After an especially irate outburst on Lucy's part, we decided to evaluate realistically how the chores were distributed. When we totalled up the household responsibilities, we found that she was indeed doing a disproportionate amount of the work. The rest of us were coasting along in the slip stream of her domestic activity. We had it made.

In our subsequent discussion we concluded that we needed to share the work and responsibilities of the family in a more equitable manner. A long period of negotiation followed, in which we redistributed the jobs among the four of us (mother, father, and two daughters). We anticipated the next week with a new perspective on the problem.

When we sat down at the dinner table the next Sunday, we were fairly well satisfied with the new arrangement. That is, everybody except twelve-year-old Shannon, our youngest daughter.

"What's the matter, Shannon?" someone asked as we observed her scowl.

"This isn't a family any more. It's a business," she replied.

"What makes you think it's a business?"

"Because everything's changed."

"You sound like you don't like the changes," Lucy probed.

"I don't."

"Why not? What don't you like?"

Initially, we assumed that the changes she didn't like involved her mother's different roles and the fact that the responsibility for the family had been distributed more equitably. That was certainly true, but only in part. After more discussion the truth came out.

"Are you afraid that we won't do what you want us to do?" we asked. Shannon's eyes filled with tears. We had hit on the problem.

"Yes. I'm afraid that you won't follow my directions because I'm just a kid." It was true. She was the youngest and the "baby" of the family. Everybody told her what to do. Very few times did we give her the power to tell us what to do.

"Shannon. The rules that apply to you also apply to us. If you're the boss in the kitchen (she was in charge of kitchen clean up after evening meals), then you're in charge. You're the boss."

"Really?"

"Yes, really."

The tears dried and her spirit lifted.

The next morning, on the kitchen refrigerator, we were met with a signed notice.

"Attention, all workers in the kitchen . . . ." What followed were ten or so rules which we were expected to follow from that day forward. Her notice was a test of our word.

Especially important, at the end of the notice, was her signature. The manifesto ended with "Shannon Guernsey, Kitchen Manager."

We were on notice that she was operating at level two of the process of power in the family. Not only were the duties in the kitchen to be distributed (i.e., who does what?), but she was asserting her prerogative about who would decide who does what.

What began as an emotional outburst on Lucy's part concerning her feelings about being overworked ended after several weeks with a new family perspective on the distribution of power. Both responsibility and prerogative were more equitably distributed. Our family was never the same after that, and neither were we as individuals. Certainly, Shannon was never the same.

THE POWER OF "WHERE"

Several years ago we were leading a weekend family seminar using the categories of energy, space, and time as a means of stimulating discussion among our audience. At the end of the morning session a well-tailored woman in her mid-forties approached us with the following question: "What if the power to control the space in the family is predetermined by conditions beyond the family's control?"

Our interest piqued, we asked, "In what way?"

"Well, take my family, for instance. My husband is a surgeon, and on the evenings before he is to perform surgery the next morning, he needs his rest. He retreats to our bedroom to read. The rest of the family is expected to keep quiet, even to the extent of not watching television."

"What do the rest of you do with your time?" we asked.

"The kids end up going to someone else's home most of the time, and I get involved in my projects."

"How is that arrangement working?"

"Not really well at all," she replied. "I really hate it that everybody is going their own way. We're just not a family any more."

Her problem was a dilemma at level three: who decides the rules. Her husband invoked his interpretation of the rules of the medical profession and consequently demanded that the family follow. Who could argue with his reasoning, especially if it involved issues of life and death?

"How is this kind of problem handled by the other families of surgeons you know?" we asked.

"I don't know. I've never thought much about it. I just assumed that's the way it is in surgeons' families." She left the seminar that afternoon with a new set of questions swirling in her mind.

The next day, a Sunday morning, after Dennis had preached in the worship service of the church, the surgeon's wife approached us again. She was eager to continue our discussion.

"Yesterday, after I got home from your seminar, I asked my husband about the rules we were using when it came to nighttime activities at our house. At first, he was defensive. But after I told him that I was going to call his fellow surgeons' wives and ask what they did, he didn't protest. So I called them. Do you know what I found out?"

"No. What?"

"I called five of my friends whose spouses use the same hospital as my husband's. Not a single one of them did what we do. In fact, when I told them what we did, three of them hinted that I was out of my mind for letting it all go on for so many years. When I reported my research to my husband, I expected him to get angry. I thought that would stop the discussion from going any further. Instead, he got a little smile on his face and said, 'I guess my game's up, isn't it?'

"I could have shot him. All these years, all this distance in the family, and for what? Just so he could have his evenings the way he wanted them. To my surprise, he agreed to let me bring the matter up with the children and to let them have a say about how evenings should be spent at our house. I couldn't believe my ears."

What had happened between this woman and her husband was a discussion at level three of the issue regarding power and space. Even though the surgeon was in most respects a fair and giving husband and father, he had been exercising his power in the family at level two — who decides who does what.

His wife moved the discussion to level three and challenged him about who decides when the rules can or should be changed.

To her surprise, and to his credit, he was amenable to the discussion. Our impression, after she left us that Sunday morning, was that their family would never quite be the same. Something had changed other than how loud the television or radio could be played in the evenings. They had negotiated an issue at a deeper level with far greater significance. They had dealt with the issue of family power.

What else can be said about the issue of space and power in a family? The most-often-asked question by parents of adolescents when we speak in public is about "the room."

Every parent of teenagers seems to know what we mean when we refer to "the room." However, most parents think the issues are those of cleanliness and neatness. Never! The issue has to do with the interaction between the phenomena of space and power.

Whose room or space is it, anyway? Is it the mother's space and she's lending it to her teenager until he or she leaves and moves out on his or her own? If so, well and good. However, if it's the teenager's room, then, who will control it? What most adolescents are saying to their parents is that they want some control of their lives, beginning with their own space. The wise parent recognizes "the room" for what it is and negotiates carefully. The unwise parent gets into a power struggle and, more often than not, wins the battle of the room but loses the war of independence. In their battle for control the teenager will "win" even at the expense of his or her own good.

Remember the illustration of the family with the daughter on drugs? The family hadn't negotiated the rules and responsibilities of power in the family. The daughter exerted her independence in a destructive and hurtful way by turning to drugs in defiance of her parents' orders. In winning, she lost.

THE POWER OF "WHEN"

The third resource in the family is time. Time has to do with the hours of the day and the months of the year.

For example, in terms of a family's eating habits, who determines when the evening meal will be served? Does it begin only after Dad gets home from work? Or does it wait for anyone in the family who is late, and under what circumstances? Have you solved the problem by eating separately, each at his or her own time?

Someone in the family wears the family's watch that determines when time begins and ends for the family. Others may own a watch but usually one person in particular wears "the" family watch.

Several years ago when Dennis began teaching at Fuller Seminary, we lived 45 freeway miles away from the school. Depending on when he left Pasadena in the afternoon, the trip home could run anywhere from an hour to an hour and a half.

During his first year of commuting, he got into the habit of waiting later and later in the afternoon to get on the freeway. The agreed-upon time for our evening meal was 6:30 P.M., but gradually, because he wore the family's watch, it drifted later and later into the evening. Often it would be 7:00 or 7:30 P.M. before he pulled into the driveway. Meanwhile, after 6:30 P.M. the kids became crankier and crankier. By the time the meal started, the troops would be in full rebellion, snapping at each other like dogs over a bone.

Finally, Lucy could take it no longer, and she made her case. It just wasn't fair to the kids or to her. Dinner would start at 6:30 P.M. The meal could be at a different time if there was a special reason or by special request. Dennis would no longer arbitrarily wear the family's watch.

The dilemma, in our case, was the agreed-upon value of eating at least one daily meal together as a family. That meal had always been in the evening.

Dennis's inability to get home on time was sabotaging our tradition.

During the first week of the new arrangement, Dennis thought about the problem and what was really at stake. He had to admit that not leaving work earlier in the afternoon was often because he allowed others to determine for him when he would leave. A meeting would run late. A client would reschedule. Someone would drop by.

What occurred to him was that Lucy and the kids had the right to expect him to submit himself to their lives simply because they were — because they existed — and their presence made a legitimate demand upon him. He had been allowing them to be displaced in the priorities of his life by responding to the demands of others. The arena of the displacement had to do with the resource of time.

Once Dennis recognized what was happening, it was amazing how he could get home on time for dinner. If a faculty meeting ran late, he simply got up and left. He began to say "no" to clients who wanted to re-schedule their appointments to the very late afternoon. He would excuse himself from those who "dropped by." His time belonged to his family.

For the most part, the family didn't realize what was happening, except for Lucy. Somehow she and Dennis had managed to negotiate a significant issue, and when it came to the resource of "time," life was smoother.

MIXING THE THREE

The interaction between power (who does what, who decides who does what, and who decides when the rules can be changed) and the resources of energy, space, and time (what, where, and when) are among the most important issues a family must negotiate in order for health and wholeness to exist.

An example of this interaction is a story shared by one of Dennis's students. The student's parents were married in the late 1950s, just prior to the young husband's decision to move to Oregon where he had been accepted in a doctoral program in clinical psychology. His wife reluctantly agreed to the move even though it involved leaving the area where her family had lived for three generations. She had lived nowhere else. (Analyzed in the vocabulary of this chapter, going to graduate school = energy; living in Oregon = space; controlling the "what" and the "where" = power).

Within three months of leaving East Texas, the student's wife returned "home" from Oregon because of severe allergies, which were attributed to her body's reaction to the dampness of the Oregon climate. She apparently reacted strongly to the mildew and fungus of the rich, but wet, Oregon environment. She seized control of the energy and space, thus reasserting her power.

Three months later the young husband returned as well, abandoning his academic plans. Instead, he took a position in his wife's family's retail furniture business. Now a dispirited and broken person (without power), he subsequently gave up any hope of fulfilling his dreams as an academic. He and his wife settled in and settled down. Her allergies passed, but his subtle-but-pervasive depression began. Fifteen years later he would be hospitalized in Dallas for severe depression with overtones of suicide.

In her discussion of the dynamics of her family genogram, Dennis's student had assumed that power in her traditional, male-dominant family rested with her father. Her mother had been the typical stay-at-home, "submissive" wife and mother who doted on her children and seemed to cater to her husband's every request.

Only when the daughter began to probe the six-month hiatus of doctoral work in Oregon did she begin to understand her father's depression and her mother's power. The father was free to do whatever he wanted, wherever he wanted, and whenever he wanted as long as he did it in East Texas near his wife's enmeshed family. He had the appearance, but not the reality, of power in the family.

His repayment was a dutiful and submissive wife who devoted herself to him and to the children. His costs were the loss of his dreams, and the progressive erosion of the joy in his life, leading finally to a vague suicide attempt and an eight-week hospitalization.

When Dennis's student approached her parents at Christmas with her insight regarding power in the family, her mother dismissed the idea out of hand. As far as the mother was concerned, "you can never trust psychology anyway." She preferred to "stick to the teachings of the Bible."

The father's response was quite the opposite. He began to open himself to his daughter for the first time in her life. He had never been more expressive and vulnerable with her.

When the student returned from Christmas break, she sensed that she had gained a new friend in her father, but she still had "the same old mother." In the process the student became aware of two of her own "birthmarks," her dependency and her tendency to manipulate others. She made the decision to become a transitional person.

THE POWER OF SERVICE

Earlier in this chapter, we suggested that power isn't always determined by the traditional categories of gender, age, status, etc. Now, as we conclude, we would like to speak to the issue of *empowerment: the responsibility and opportunity for those who have power to release it to others so that they may become equals.*

The responsibility of whoever has the power in a family, a church, a community, a nation, or in any other human institution, is to serve those with lesser power. We serve them by sharing our power and leading them into a position of equality.

This empowerment follows the example of Jesus, "who, although He existed in the form of God, did not regard equality with God a thing to be grasped, but emptied Himself, taking the form of a bond-servant . . ." (Phil. 2:5 ff., NASB).

Whoever is the head of the family, the church, the community, or the nation has the greater responsibility to serve those of lesser position. That person is responsible to empower others, to build them up, until they are equals and are invested with the ability to empower others in turn.

Much of the contemporary dysfunction in our families, in our churches, in our communities, and in our nation would be ameliorated, even eliminated, if we, like Christ, would empower others rather than cling to the power for ourselves. Transitional people take the risk of empowering others, of giving away their resources in service to others.

10.

An Adaptive Solution

One of the greatest challenges of parenting is living with the chaos children sometimes create. For example, each of our three naturally born children came into the world with his or her own kind of spontaneity, or disorderliness.

Our first child, a son, came into the world in the middle of the night, prefaced by our walking the streets of our Dallas neighborhood because of Lucy's discomfort. At first it didn't occur to us that she had begun labor. When we realized what was happening, we drove post-haste to the hospital.

Several hours later, after Stephen was born, as Dennis walked out of the recovery room, the head nurse asked, "Well, Mr. Guernsey, how is Mrs. Guernsey?"

Innocently and naively, Dennis replied, "She's doing well, thank you. She had a fairly easy time of it."

The veteran nurse rose up from her chair behind the nurses' station, waving her finger in his face. With a firm voice she said, "Young man, it may have been quick, but it's never easy, and don't you ever forget it."

Appropriately chastised, Dennis breathlessly mumbled something and stumbled out of the hospital. He's never forgotten her rebuke. Childbirth may be quick but it's never easy. It's certainly not easy physically, and it's not easy emotionally. A new life inevitably imposes the need for adaptation and change.

Our second child, a daughter, was born in the labor room with her umbilical cord wrapped around her neck, Lucy calling for help, Dennis running out to the same nurses' station, this time yelling for the doctors and nurses to "do something." Sheryl was a complicated surprise from the very beginning.

Our third was born so quickly (Lucy's entreaties to the labor room nurse having gone unheeded) that the obstetrician was late. Running into the delivery room, hopping on one foot, he frantically pulled on his surgical gown and booties as our second daughter simultaneously arrived more or less on her own. As Dennis looked on from a distance, staff personnel were running around the delivery room like Keystone Cops, preparing Lucy for birth even as it was happening. It was as if Shannon was born saying, "Ready or not, here I come!"

The very nature of childbirth isn't neat and tidy. The event is messy and painful, as if to remind us that life with our children may often be like that as well — "quick, but never easy." Children, families, and life itself, are rarely neat, tidy, and organized on their own. Why? Because of the nature of the people and the processes involved.

Think of the time and energy spent trying to get what is messy or untidy clean, straight and ordered. How many arguments, how many fights, how much conflict can there be in trying to agree on a standard?

Suppose a young man and a young woman marry. What attracts him to her is a combination of her physical beauty and her approach to life. She's a practical, down-to-earth kind of woman. What attracts her to him is the excitement he brings to her life. He loves adventure and approaches life as if risks are opportunities rather than barriers. Together they make a great combination.

However, within three months of their marriage they're in trouble. Mostly, she's dissatisfied. He misses work if the waves are up and the surfing looks good. In her opinion, he's without ambition. He seems to do whatever he "feels like doing," even if he is scheduled to work or has made a prior commitment.

Living with him is a disaster, according to her. He comes home from work, steps out of his dirty clothes and leaves them heaped in the middle of the bedroom, waiting for her to come through and pick them up. The distance from where he leaves his mess to the clothes hamper is less than six feet. Her reminders have taken on the sound of a bill collector's complaint. "Nag, nag, nag."

According to him, life with her is like living with a drill sergeant. She's "never satisfied." Nothing he does or tries "ever" pleases her. Her demands are endless, as are her standards. Everything seems scheduled, with no room for change. It seems as if there is a "right way" and a "wrong way" to hang clothes, to choose a movie, to eat, to talk, to think. He's come to the conclusion that "you can't satisfy her, so have a good time." Life's too short and the waves won't last.

What they need in their relationship (and what is needed if unhealthy generational "birthmarks" are to be removed successfully) is the capacity for adaptability, the ability of a relationship to flex, to change the rules by which it operates — that is, the capacity of a relationship to flex while maintaining some degree of continuity.

That's a pretty formal definition. Let's see if we can lighten it up a bit.

In the case of this young couple, their relationship will be in trouble over the long haul if they don't learn the rules for negotiating change. They are focusing on the clothes or the nagging rather than on what they can do to adapt if one or the other of them isn't happy or is dissatisfied.

Remember, power has to do with who decides how or when to change. Adaptability has to do with how change itself is managed.

In order to envision adaptation, we think in terms of a continuum.

Chaos	*Flexibility*	*Rigidity*

At one end of the continuum is chaos or complete disorder. At the other end is rigidity or inflexible order. In the middle is flexibility, the quality of suppleness or compliance.

Too much adaptability can lead to chaos. A statement in the Old Testament, "and everyone did what was right in his own eyes" (Judg. 21:25) is descriptive. In that account, the people of Israel lived as if each person or tribe was the source for its own rules. There was no leadership, no order. Each person was a rule unto himself.

The young husband in our opening illustration is an example of someone who wants to "do what is right in his own eyes." He is an example of someone who lives on the chaotic end of the continuum, although he would define his approach as "freedom." However, the situation he creates, one without accountability and without structure, tends toward chaos.

In contrast, for his new wife security comes from fixed rules and expectations. "A place for everything and everything in its place" is the plaque hung on the wall of her perception of the world. The world she creates, one with fixed and uncompromising standards, is characterized by rigidity and inflexibility.

If both of these partners insist on their own way and neither is willing to change, conflict is certain, and discouragement and incompatibility are inevitable.

HOW TO CHANGE

We suggest the following seven principles as a means of facilitating the ability to change and to fit in with one another's idiosyncrasies. As you read, think of your two families—your generational family and the family you're in now. How did they and how do they handle change? Your observations will provide a mirror for reflection on and understanding of the "birthmarks" you carry regarding your ability to handle change.

1. Remember, Things Are Rarely "Right or Wrong"

The question of change seldom can be reduced to a moral issue. Words like "good" and "bad," "right" and "wrong" expose the need to couch our opinions as absolutes.

For example, a conflict between Dennis and Lucy during their first year of marriage was about the towels in the bathroom. They both agreed that the towels needed to be hung up after use. They didn't agree on how they should be folded. Dennis folded them in half, the more economical movement, and Lucy folded them in thirds, the more aesthetic solution. Further, she wanted all the towels hung the same way — her way!

A different way of doing things was reduced to an argument about who was "right" and who was "wrong." In the midst of the fight, Dennis sarcastically remarked something to the effect of "and God created towels on the fifth day and said, 'Let them be folded in thirds.'" The argument degenerated from that point onward.

Later, after things had cooled off, we were able to discuss the issue beyond the assumptions of right and wrong. The issue seemed to be one of what the relative importance was to whom and why. We agreed that the matter of the towels was definitely more important to Lucy than it was to Dennis. The adjustment in his standard would be minor, so he adjusted. To this day we still fold the towels in the bathroom into thirds before returning them to the rack. They are now a reminder of how relatively minor differences become major conflicts.

Of course, there are moral absolutes such as "thou shalt not kill," "thou shalt not commit adultery," etc. However, "men shall not wear their hair at shoulder length" does not qualify as an absolute, even though we know of families that have been torn asunder over the length of hair, the wearing of makeup, pierced ears, and similar concerns. Rather than having been alienated from one another over absolutes, these families have pulled apart over differences in lifestyles, personal preferences, convictions, social proprieties, or ideologies—issues that are negotiable and not absolute. The key is to distinguish what is negotiable from what is not and to flex unless there is a concrete, unequivocal reason for not negotiating.

2. Find An Adaptive Solution

In your communication regarding change, look for a creative solution that satisfies the concerns or objections of both of you.

When we moved into our present home about ten years ago, we agreed that as a part of the remodeling of the place, we would install a hot tub. The house is all redwood, and the thought of a redwood hot tub in the backyard appealed to us both.

Dennis proceeded to draw up a design for the backyard, done to scale, identifying where the tub should be placed. He took his drawing in hand and approached Lucy.

"Here's the design for the backyard," he declared, spreading the plot plan before her.

"What's this?" she asked.

"That's the hot tub," he replied.

"I don't want it there," she stated, arguing that it would be too close to the neighbor's yard.

"You decided about the inside of the house. I'll decide about the outside," Dennis countered, emotion surfacing in his voice. They were clearly talking about two different issues.

"Well, I don't agree with your decision, and I especially don't like where you want to put the hot tub." Lucy hunched her shoulders in resistance.

"Great! That's just great!" Dennis yelled as he wadded up the carefully drawn-to-scale plan and threw it on the table. With that fit of pique there was a retreat to the backyard where there began a vigorous and sustained argument over the positioning of the hot tub.

After what seemed like several hours of negotiating (it was probably only an hour or so), from the inside of the house came a plaintive suggestion. Our daughter Shannon had grown weary of our conflict. "Why don't you put the hot tub here?" She pointed to a spot neither of us had considered. Her suggestion pointed to a new way of approaching the problem and gave us a new set of assumptions and guidelines. Within minutes we had reconfigured our backyard plan and had incorporated her suggestion.

If you were to visit us today, you would find the hot tub sitting in the place Shannon suggested. It's as if it belongs there and nowhere else. We had found an adaptive solution.

This suggestion is a necessary corollary to the first. When you don't have a moral absolute, a right or wrong to appeal to, then you have to reach your solution via some other route.

We suggest adaptation and flexibility. Look first for a solution that satisfies both of you completely, but be ready to accept a solution that may not satisfy either of you completely but does satisfy the essence of the issues as best as you can define them.

Our hot tub stands as a constant reminder to us of an adaptive solution and the benefit of innovation and reconfiguration, even if it takes outside help.

3. Don't Quit!

Many arguments end in bitterness or frustration rather than satisfaction or resolution because the participants quit too soon or too easily. Conflict is hard work. Many of us don't want to put forth the effort required to find an adaptive solution. It often seems easier to roll over and let the other person have his or her own way.

However, nothing can sabotage a relationship more in the long run than false or phony accord. One day the differences will show up in another place, at another time, or over another issue. When that time comes, it's as if the person who has given up and given in over the years empties his or her gunny sack of past accommodations all over the place. Then, rather than arguing about where to put the hot tub, the conflict may turn into a discussion over whether or not to continue the marriage or the relationship.

4. Don't Bully!

The opposite of quitting too soon and letting the other person have his or her own way is the pattern of bullying. Sometimes when we're losing an argument, it's tempting to shift gears and use intimidation—to become a bully.

An adaptive solution doesn't come from the person who can yell the loudest, get the most angry, or utter the strongest insult. Neither does it depend on which person is the most verbal and the most adept at argumentation.

Rather, an adaptive solution is a function of respect for the opinion of the other and a commitment to the process of problem-solving. Yelling, threats, and insults are like weapons of war that needlessly escalate a conflict. If you're not going to quit, you also have to commit yourself to be reasonable in the often long and arduous process en route to a solution.

5. Observe the Principle That Nothing Breaks That Can't Be Fixed

Change isn't necessarily permanent. If you change something and it doesn't work, you can always change it back again. Very few decisions, very few settlements, are of such a nature that they can't be amended and altered. Changes can be changed.

Similarly, when there is a disruption in a relationship, most of the time what appears to be irreconcilably broken can be fixed.

That's been Dennis's experience in over twenty-five years of doing therapy. The irony of much of marital and family therapy is that relationships which by all estimates should not work because of the level of dysfunction do work because of the participants' willingness to change and accept responsibility for the work involved. Relationships that should work out sometimes don't, because of the unwillingness of the participants to change and the tendency to put individual agendas ahead of relational ones.

What seems to make a difference is an *internal attitude* of flexibility on the part of marital partners or family members. The willingness to adapt for the good of the relationship is what sees people through the tough times of conflict and dissonance. A conviction that brokenness isn't a permanent state is what buoys them through the hard work needed to bring about change.

6. Make Unity, Not Uniformity, Your Goal

It's more important to be of one spirit than to be of one kind. It's more important to be of one mind than to think the same thoughts. Too many people confuse uniformity with unity. Unity embraces diversity and difference. Uniformity suggests conformity and same-ness. In terms of the continuum, flexibility assumes a commitment to unity, rigidity assumes a commitment to uniformity, and chaos assumes no commitment at all.

We recall the illustration used by the late, respected theologian Francis Schaeffer. He was asked during the radical non-conformist 1960s what he would do if a young person showed up barefooted for Sunday services. To the surprise of his audience, Dr. Schaeffer responded that he would probably take his own shoes off rather than exclude the young person. He argued for an inclusive spirit of unity rather than an exclusive spirit of unifor-mity, an idea that was foreign to his audience at the time.

A spirit of unity, when it comes to relationships, assures the participants that their uniqueness will not get lost in the shuffle. It assures participants that minority status, for whatever reason, won't exclude them from the process of making decisions. A spirit of unity emulates the mind of Christ in that it places an empha-sis upon inclusion rather than exclusion, upon diversity rather than conformity.

7. Remember, Not Everything Is Negotiable

Human beings are created in the image of God, and that means they are created to be in relationship with one another. Whatever violates or defaces that image is not and cannot be in the will of God.

Suppose, for example, a husband suggests to his wife that she participate with him in mate-swapping. On the way to a party he informs her that he wants to pick out one of the other women and to retreat to one of the bedrooms and have sex with her. She is free to do the same with any of the other men she meets. She protests. He insists.

At the party, he makes his move and she complies, seething inside at the humiliation. What happens at the party settles into a lifestyle. They have an open marriage in which either partner is free to engage in sexual activities with whomever he or she wants.

At a later date, she decides she can't stand this way of life any more and wants out of the marriage. When he resists and suggests counseling, she responds that he has to live with the situation he created. Her anger and bitterness focus upon his original suggestion. Though she participated, she blames him for the deterioration of their relationship, pointing to the night the mate-swapping began.

Whether it be sexual infidelity, sexual or physical abuse, or habitual neglect, the integrity and dignity of another person cannot be violated without the expectation that the violation will produce extreme results. The essential dignity and integrity of a human being is not negotiable, nor is the essential dignity and integrity of a relationship between two humans. Moral absolutes exist for the protection of the person who has been created in the image of God. The dignity and integrity of that creation cannot be negotiated away.

SUMMING UP

As you think through what we've said in this chapter, reflect upon your generational family. On the whole, do you see a family that has been operating at either of the extremes of the adaptability continuum, chaos or rigidity? If so, what patterns or "birthmarks" can you identify that emerge from those positions?

Now read again the suggestions for managing

change, but this time from the perspective of a transitional person. The list is not intended to be exhaustive, so feel free to add other suggestions as they occur to you. What's of consequence to us is that a transitional person becomes an agent of change within his or her family system. Remember, more often than not an agent of change experiences resistance and dissatisfaction as a matter of course. So, don't quit. That's what God's grace is for. It's for the times we want to quit but can't, when we want to stop but won't.

11.

The Hidden Geometry of the Family

Although most of us learned in high school that "the shortest distance between two points is a straight line," when it comes to our closest relationships we often live as if "the only way to communicate to one person is through another." We habitually take the longer, more indirect route. In literature on the family this pattern of communication is called "triangling."

The story of the Andrews family illustrates what we mean.

Nancy Andrews, wife and mother, is a try-hard, intense forty-year-old woman who is known in her family for her illnesses. She is particularly noted for her allergic reaction to almost everything. As a child her allergies were serious but not debilitating. However, once she was married, they surfaced with a vengeance.

As our story begins, she is under her physician's care following a reaction to a drug he had prescribed as a part of her ongoing battle with her medical problems.

Nelson Andrews, husband and father, is an unemotional, inexpressive man who is forty-five years old. He works as a salesman for an auto parts distributor and has reached the top of his earning potential in that position. He is famous for his laconic responses to his wife's physical ailments. He has been known to stop at the neighborhood market for snacks and magazines on his way to the emergency room with his wife, who was having a life-threatening attack of asthma.

Married for twenty years, they have two children, ages fifteen and seventeen. The elder, a daughter, is "daddy's favorite." She is bright, verbal, and attractive. In his eyes, she can do no wrong. She is the star of the family. The youngest, a son, is pampered by his mother whenever she's not ill. Much of the time, however, she demands that the son look after her needs, a task she says her husband and her daughter refuse to do. The son has learned to manipulate his mother, using her dependence on him as his tool. His relationship with his father and sister is distant and cool.

Central, as well, to the Andrews' family story are Nancy's parents. Her 63-year-old father is an alcoholic. Miraculously, he has been able to keep the same job for forty years even though there are days when he is barely capable of performing his work. His supervisor, a drinking buddy of thirty years (a co-alcoholic) has learned to cover for him. His 62-year-old wife, Nancy's mother, is an anxious person who nervously flits from person to person, telling each of her worries and her woes, especially her complaints about her marriage. She is notorious for talking on the telephone for hours, especially to her married daughters, all of whom except for Nancy have moved away from the area.

If you were diagramming the Andrews family, including the grandparents, you would identify the following overly close coalitions: Nancy and her son, Nelson and his daughter, Nancy and her mother, Nancy's mother and each of Nancy's sisters. The odd man out is the grandfather who smoozes with his buddies at work and is the topic of much of the gossip between the grandmother and her daughters.

Likewise, if you were to listen to the communication system of the family at any given moment, you would hear them complaining about one another but not *to* one another. Each person talks to his or her confidant as if he or she was the only one in the world. The rumors, innuendoes, and gossip travel faster than the speed of light (that is, as fast as the signals on the phone lines can take them). Someone is usually angry at someone else, but that someone else rarely knows about it until later, if ever. If the matter is brought up face to face, the complainant typically denies or discounts the rumor.

As a result, conflict between persons is rarely direct but is exhibited instead through backbiting and gossip. The emotional distance between family members is breached only at times of crisis associated with physical illness. Feelings, especially anger, are repressed and denied. It's possible for the whole family to be together on holidays and never discuss how they actually feel about one another. The hurt and anger surface over the phone in the days following the family get-together. By talking to a confidant and not talking to the person with whom he or she is upset, the pattern of the triangle forms. This is the hidden geometry of the family.

Triangling, the patterns of coalitions within and between relationships, allows for the appearance of closeness and togetherness without the reality of intimacy. Secretly, most members of the Andrews family carry a grudge against somebody, never thinking that someone carries a grudge against them.

Nancy feels sick and fearful. Nelson feels trapped and resentful. Each of their children, isolated in his or her own way, works at staying away from home. Quietly, the seventeen-year-old daughter is counting the days until she graduates from high school and can go away to college. The son, unknown to his parents, has begun to experiment with marijuana with his friends. When confronted with this information by the parents of one of their son's friends, Nancy and Nelson deny his actions. He lies about his drug use, and they reassure their son that they would never believe such rumors about him.

At first glance, this story sounds bleak and foreboding, but upon further examination its classic nature can be seen to be fairly typical and treatable. The triangles are clear and persistent though often hurtful and destructive.

TYPES OF TRIANGLES

Let's take a look at how the Andrews family evidences three of the most common patterns of family triangling. As we describe each "birthmark," see if you can identify which pattern your generational family tends to use. Then, ask yourself about the relationships you're now in.

Two Against One

The phenomenon of "ganging up" is illustrative of the relationships between Nancy and her mother against her father. It's probably true of the relationship between Nancy and her son against Nelson.

The pattern can be diagrammed as such,

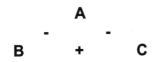

If the grandfather is A, and Nancy's grandmother is B, then whomever she recruits to be on her side against her alcoholic husband is C. All of the phone calls, all of the comforting of the mother, all of the complaining, even when justified, between B and C will not change the relationship between A and B. The triangling allows the grandmother to vent her feelings against her husband without negotiating through them with him.

Similarly, the pattern between Nelson (A) and Nancy (B) and their fifteen-year-old son (C) repeats this pattern. Nancy is able to talk to her son about her husband and thus avoid the direct discomfort and anger she feels toward him.

In terms of our own family, this pattern existed between Sheryl (B) and Dennis (C) against Lucy (A). Beginning when Sheryl was about age nine or ten and lasting for seven or eight years, Dennis began to allow himself to be triangled by Sheryl against Lucy. The three of us have since talked about the pattern and we agree that Lucy was the "odd person out." When Sheryl would come to Dennis with her complaints about Lucy,

Dennis would listen patiently and try to "explain" Lucy to her. Believing at the time that he was doing a good thing, he would attempt to deflect Sheryl's hurt and anger.

Not once did his willingness to listen to Sheryl's frustration improve the relationship between her and her mother. In fact, he pretty much agreed with Sheryl's complaints, and the triangling allowed him to avoid addressing the issues with Lucy.

Finally, after an especially stressful argument between Sheryl and Lucy, and after being confronted by Lucy, Dennis realized what he was doing. He wasn't making things better; he was making them worse.

When Sheryl approached him the next time, he said he would not listen to her complaints and that she needed to work it out with her mother. Sheryl was incredulous. Her source of sympathy had dried up. She flounced off in a huff, muttering under her breath that "no one cared or understood."

What began that day was a long and sometimes painful process of reconciliation between a teenage daughter and her mother. Without meaning to, Dennis had gotten in the way of the process between them. After he and Sheryl stopped "ganging up" against Lucy, the family prospered accordingly.

Two After One

The pattern that probably exists between Nancy (B) and Nelson (C) and their eldest daughter (A) is called "two after one," and can be diagrammed as follows:

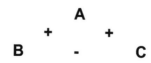

In this pattern Nancy and Nelson compete for the favor and approval of their daughter. The daughter is given inordinate control. She holds the power of blessing.

For example, this pattern often occurs in a relationship between a divorced couple and their children. The mother typically has custody throughout the week and the father has them one or two weekends a month. Because she is functioning as the disciplinarian during the week, the mother is placed in a tenuous position. On the weekend when he has the children, the father is able to smother them with goodies the mother can't afford. He spoils them with gifts and attention. When they return to their mother's custody they chatter on and on about the good time they had, about the places they went, about the money he spent.

With or without realizing it, the mother can be drawn into a pattern of competition with the father for the approval of the children. The mother spends money on toys she can't afford. She lets the kids stay up and watch TV later than she normally would because their father lets them when they're with him. She becomes permissive about chores and responsibilities. The children learn to play the parents against each other.

In terms of the Andrews family, the irony is that although the daughter appears to "win" (i.e., her parents compete for her favor), actually, she loses in at least two ways.

First of all, she loses because her "investment" in their marriage is sabotaged by their pursuit of her. No child, down deep inside, wants to win anything at the expense of the relationship that created her. When a couple gives a child that kind of power, the child takes it, uses it, and, eventually, comes to resent her parents for giving it to her.

Second, she loses because she becomes accustomed to an unwarranted position of privilege. She garners a level of prestige that is unrealistic and unreasonable. It's ultimately hurtful to her to be given power to determine her parents' self-esteem. Later in life she will expect others to defer to her as did her parents. She will expect others to pursue her as did her mother and father. When others don't, or won't, she will feel diminished. Her expectations regarding relationships will be tilted immoderately toward her. She will be disappointed when things don't work out her way. Others might consider her to be selfish and self-centered. She is clearly losing a lot.

Two For One

On the surface, the pattern of "two for one," diagrammed below, would appear to be desirable and helpful.

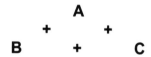

In fact, it can be either helpful or hurtful. It's hurtful when the pattern is closed and the positive valences among the family members are used against another. What we mean can be diagrammed as

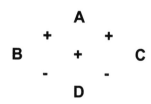

The coalition of A, B, and C unites against whomever or whatever D represents.

For example, Dennis remembers a friend in high school whose parents thought he could do no wrong. He was an only child born late in their marriage. They had accustomed themselves to being childless when his mother became pregnant. As the apple of his parents' eye, he learned, even in elementary school, to play off his parents against whomever stood in his way. Whether it was his teachers, law enforcement, or any other form of authority, by the time he was in high school he had convinced his mother and father that the world was against him and, therefore, against them.

During his senior year in high school he participated in the armed robbery of a nearby liquor store. He was recognized by one of the patrons, arrested, tried, and convicted. His parents fought his conviction with all of their resources, eventually coming near bankruptcy in his support. Throughout the trial he told his parents he was innocent, and they believed him. Only to one of his friends did he admit his guilt. When he was imprisoned in the California Youth Authority, his parents were crushed. Years later we learned that he had been sent to prison for life, as a habitual offender.

The alliance or coalition among the three of them was closed. The bond between them prohibited relationships with anyone outside the family. Relationships outside the coalition were seen as threats and were to be resisted. In his case the "two for one" proved to be destructive and hurtful.

The "two for one" pattern is helpful when a coalition is formed on behalf of someone who cannot defend or protect him / herself. Such might be the case of parents going to the aid of their child against the bureaucracy of a school if the child is unable to get the educational system to be responsive. Other such interventions on the behalf of legitimate victims are appropriate.

BIBLICAL ALTERNATIVES

An alternative to triangling is the formation of what family therapy literature calls a "triad." A triad is a relationship among three persons that is open rather than closed. Coalitions, if they exist, are "out on top of the table" rather than covert and under the table. In a triad, the participants talk to one another rather than about one another. Using a Biblical example, if they "have aught against another, they go to him" (cf. Matt. 18:15).

Rather than playing one against another, or the whole of the triangle against the world, they place service to one another as a priority (cf. Matt. 20:20 ff.). They take seriously Jesus' teaching to love your enemies rather than hate them.

And, last of all, the pattern of "two for one" is helpful when it brings empowerment to the weak, until they can become strong in and of themselves.

The writer of the Old Testament book of Ecclesiastes wrote,

> Two are better than one,
>> because they have a good return for their work;
> If one falls down,
>> his friend can help him up;
> But pity the man who falls
>> and has no one to help him up!
> . . . .
> Though one may be overpowered,
>> two can defend themselves.
> A cord of three strands is not quickly broken.
>> (Eccl. 4:10-12, NIV)

FURTHER IMPLICATIONS

The difference between a triangle and a triad has far-reaching implications for our contemporary world. Take, for example, the habit in church for the people of God to criticize and condemn one another rather than confront one another face to face. How many church fights or church splits have been the consequence of triangling? How many bruised feelings? How many depressed, discouraged and disgruntled believers have been objects of a two-against-one triangle?

Second, how many times do we set up our leaders in a two-for-one triangle to expect our competition among ourselves for their favor? How many of their egos need to be stroked to such an extent that we compete for their favor like supplicants before the throne of royalty? The end result, so common in recent years, is the shattered reputations of Christian superstars who have lost contact with their humanity. We believe, and they believe, that they are different.

Finally, how frequently do we huddle together in hurtful two-for-one triangles, like terrified children waiting for the end of the world or the coming of Armageddon? How often do we communicate to our young that the world is a frightening place and that they are in constant danger? How often in our fearfulness do we foster anxiety rather than faith?

Who would ever think that the basic problem might have something to do with the geometry of human relationships?

As a transitional person, commit yourself to the following:

1. Talk to one another rather than about one another.
2. Refuse to gossip about others. Instead, "speak the truth, one to another."
3. Place service to others as a priority rather than indulge in backbiting and criticism.
4. Empower the weak to become strong, whenever possible.

12.

The Life and Times of a Transitional Person

Caleb was a crusty, wizened, curmudgeonly kind of man when at the end of his life he finally laid claim to his inheritance in the land of Canaan, as promised by Moses. We are told in the Old Testament Book of Joshua that at eighty-five years of age he assertively demanded his due, based upon his faithfulness, his trials, and his wholehearted service to the God of Israel.

> I was forty years old when Moses the servant of the LORD sent me from Kadesh Barnea to explore the land. And I brought him back a report according to my convictions, but my brothers who went up with me made the hearts of the people melt with fear. I, however, followed the LORD my God wholeheartedly . . . .

179

Now then, just as the LORD promised, he has kept me alive for forty-five years since the time he said this to Moses, while Israel moved about in the desert. So here I am today, eighty-five years old! I am still as strong today as the day Moses sent me out . . . . *Now give me this hill country that the* LORD *promised me that day.* You yourself heard that the Anakites were there and their cities were large and fortified, but, the LORD helping me, I will drive them out just as he said (Josh. 14:7-12, NIV, emphasis added).

He would not be denied. Caleb was the quintessential transitional person.

GIVE ME THE HILL COUNTRY

Caleb is an example of a transitional person because he represents the "stick-to-it" kind of attitude that we must have in order to accomplish the work of changing generational "birthmarks." Several principles come to mind as illustrated by Caleb's life.

First, *the transitional person has experienced deliverance individually and knows that, somehow, God was involved in the process.* The irony of the experience of transitional persons is that they know in their gut that the solution to their family's problems lies in their response to God. They know, however tentatively, that Jehovah is their refuge. Their memories carry the imprint of God's active response to their cry. The story begins in their own personal Egypt, but the author and animator of the story is God.

Caleb's story began in Egypt. He knew the oppression of his Egyptian taskmasters. He had endured the humiliation of subjugation. He had experienced the daily routines of repression associated with slavery. His heart ached for freedom. Then the God of Israel moved, and Caleb became a part of God's story.

On the night of the Passover when the death angel swept through Egypt, Caleb covered his door post with the blood of sacrifice. He heard the wailing of the Egyptian mothers for the deaths of their firstborn. He understood the miracle and mercy of salvation.

Although we are not told so directly, we know he participated in the deliverance of Israel from captivity and took part in the Red Sea experience. If he had not seen, he would have heard of Moses' smiting the waters of the Red Sea with his stick and the miraculous parting of the waves. He knew of God's seaward burial of Israel's pursuers. He and thousands of his fellow travelers had climbed onto the banks of Sinai as free people. The experience must have made an indelible impression on him, one he would draw upon in the years to come.

Transitional people have both a knowledge and experience of God's deliverance. Sometimes they know the name of their redeemer directly (that is, they are followers of Christ), and at other times they refer more indirectly to God as "a higher power." For whatever reason, redemption and deliverance are a part of their experiential vocabulary.

Second, *transitional persons are often singled out by circumstances not of their own choosing.* Life has a way of positioning some people at certain decision points in the history of their family where they have both the opportunity and the felt obligation to make decisions for persons other than themselves.

We first learn of Caleb in chapter 13 of the Book of Numbers, when he is selected by Moses to represent the tribe of Judah as its agent to spy out the land of Canaan prior to Israel's invasion. Imagine his pride when his name was called out to go on behalf of the tribe of Judah. When he stepped forward, adrenalin must have been coursing through his body. Little did he know what the future held. He only knew he had been chosen to accomplish a task, his name had been called, and he would go.

A lesson to be learned from Caleb is that becoming a transitional person is nearly always an evolving, emerging experience, perhaps beginning with a romantic commitment. It involves an unfolding of circumstances which take on meaning as they happen.

Probably, as well, the lesson involves a recognition that in the beginning one can't see the end. Your name is called. You choose to go. You make the decision about where you are going, not on the basis of a fixed destination but on the basis of the faithfulness of the one who chooses you. You have to trust in the God who calls you to sort out the directions as you go. Had Caleb known what would be required of him, would he have stepped forward so patriotically? In all likelihood he would have, but perhaps not with such brazen assurance.

Third, *at the moment of decision, transitional persons are able to see what others around them cannot see.* You have chosen to be a transitional person when you have a vision for what could be rather than what is. To you, problems that bind your family, though large and ominous, do not appear insurmountable.

In Caleb's case, only he and Joshua were able to see the land of Canaan for what it was—a land of opportunity (cf. Num. 13:26-33). Their colleagues, the other ten spies who went with them, reported the same facts but with a different spin. All twelve saw the advantages of Canaan, but those ten acknowledged only the barriers and dangers.

How frustrated Caleb must have been. He was able to transpose his previous experience of deliverance into the future to believe that the God who had redeemed them from Egypt would be with them in Canaan as well. The others focused only upon current circumstances. Caleb, as a transitional person, focused upon the God who would go with them (see Num. 14:24).

So it is for the transitional person. Often, they are outvoted by the majority because the majority cannot envision the empowering presence of God in the process. Others can only see the pain and the danger. These fears force the transitional person to make another decision.

Fourth, *the transitional person chooses to remain connected to family through desert and wandering experiences rather than disconnecting and going it alone.* Caleb and Joshua must have had a conversation with one another concerning Canaan. Should they split and lead a "rump convention" (choosing their own candidate) or should they stay and suffer the consequences of the majority decision? When they chose to stay, they couldn't have known about the forty-year journey ahead. Their loyalty to their family kept them attached even in the face of God's obvious displeasure with Israel's disbelief.

Caleb was caught between two polarities: the pull of loyalty toward his tribe and the pull of obedience toward God. In the end he decided to remain with his people, suffering the indignities and discomfort of the desert while holding onto the promise of God.

The temptation faced by every transitional person is to walk away from his or her willful, stubborn, hardhearted brood and go it alone. The test of the transitional person's commitment is to stay when it would be easier to leave, to remain when it would be easier to exit.

Transitional people must decide that their willfulness and stubbornness, buoyed by the grace of God, can outlast the willfulness and stubbornness of their family.

No one would have blamed Moses, Joshua, or Caleb if they had walked out on the whole lot of their disobedient kinsmen and had started anew with God on their own. In fact, in Exodus 32, God suggests just such a scenario. God had grown weary of Israel's hardheartedness and idolatry. God had suggested that they begin again, yet Moses and the others chose to remain with their people. Their loyalty outweighed their temptation to leave, however logical and reasonable that leaving would have been.

The loyalty of transitional persons to their families is based upon their love and commitment, not upon blind and senseless masochistic duty. They can see where they are going and they can see what it will cost. They choose to stay connected and committed regardless of the hardship involved. Their solace is in the God who will go with them through the experience.

Fifth, *transitional persons remain faithful to their vision, though others along the journey fall away.* In Caleb's story, the forty years in the desert were difficult in and of themselves.

But, the greater hardship must have been the loss he both observed and experienced when his colleagues, the adults over the age of twenty at the time of their refusal to enter into Canaan, began to die. How many funerals did he attend? How many visits of comfort and condolence did he make? How often was he reminded of the consequences of his people's disobedience?

Somehow, he remained faithful to his original vision.

Likewise, the transitional person must take the long view when evaluating his or her future. In the short term, the daily consequences and costs may seem overwhelming. Sometimes, it's a lonely experience.

Caleb must have lost a lot of people he loved very dearly. For the transitional person, losses are common. People they love fall away before the end of the journey. It's during these times of loss that uncertainty and unbelief inevitably creep in. Did I make the right decision? Is it really worth it? Must I go on alone?

Then, a day comes when the "nation" chooses to do what they should have chosen to do years earlier. They make the decision to obey God and occupy the promised land. They cross over the Jordan and begin the years of conquest and victory.

Generalizing from Caleb's experience at this time, in the final push, *the transitional person chooses the more difficult and demanding obstacles to challenge and conquer.* There came a time in Caleb's life when it was time for him to reap the rewards of his faithfulness. The people of Israel had, for the most part, conquered the land, and it was time to divide the spoils.

In a remarkable speech of courage and single-mindedness, Caleb chose for himself and his family a portion of land which was as yet unsubjugated—the hill country of Hebron (cf. Josh. 14:1-15). Technically speaking, he could have chosen any part of the land, including the richest and most fertile of the valleys, for himself. Instead, at the age of eighty-five he asserted his vitality and challenged his family to follow him into battle.

The seasoned experience of transitional persons asserts itself when, in evaluating how the transitions will be managed, they choose to remain active and engaged in life. They plan to stay with the process until it is finished. Their stubbornness eventually prevails.

Last of all, *transitional persons are rewarded by God for their faithfulness, and their progeny share in the blessing perpetually.*

Some of the most encouraging verses in all of the Bible are recorded in Joshua 14:13-15 (NIV):

> Then Joshua blessed Caleb son of Jephunneh and gave him Hebron as his inheritance. So Hebron has belonged to Caleb son of Jephunneh the Kenizzite ever since, because he followed the LORD, the God of Israel, wholeheartedly. . . .
>
> Then the land had rest from war.

Caleb prevailed. The wandering ceased, as did the dying. The transience and insecurity came to an end. The fighting and the warring were over. He, his family, and his land, were able to be at rest. He had changed the course of history for his family.

The transitional person needs to know there is a place called "Hebron" for him or her. There will be a time when the battles will cease and the roses will grow in the garden again. There will be a time of peace and tranquility. The hassles will be finished and the face of life will be whole and healthy and beautiful—free from all unsightly "birthmarks."

Frequently, the only motivation keeping transitional persons going is a vision of Hebron, the place of rest for them and their family. They hope that what was true for Caleb will be true for them.

WHAT DO THESE STONES MEAN?

The process of becoming a transitional person is not a private act. There is a story that demands to be told.

Associated with the story are the names and biographies of men and women, friends and family, who lived and shared the struggle and who helped pay for the victory.

As the children of Israel crossed over the Jordan and into Canaan, the Lord told Joshua to build a memorial of their experience so that,

> in the future, when your children ask you, 'What do these stones mean?' tell them that the flow of the Jordan was cut off before the ark of the covenant of the LORD. When it crossed the Jordan, the waters of the Jordan were cut off. *These stones are to be a memorial to the people of Israel forever* (Josh. 4:6b-7, NIV, emphasis added).

We encourage you to create your own memorial, your own story to be handed down to future generations. Find others who will participate with you in the telling of your story — your children, your family, or some friends. The presence of a group that listens as you tell the story will be both an encouragement and a source of motivation for them as well as for you.

STEPS IN BUILDING A MEMORIAL

As you think in terms of your own life, what was your "Red Sea experience," your own time of redemption and deliverance? Under what conditions did the deliverance occur? Who were your fellow travelers? Who, or what, made the crossing difficult? Who, or what, made the crossing possible or smoothed the way?

Caleb's journey as a transitional person began with his redemption from Egypt and God's miraculous deliverance through the Red Sea. Your story has a beginning place too. Perhaps, the time is now for you to discover "what these stones mean."

Next, what and when have been your Sinai experiences? It's easy to disclose the good times and the fun times about ourselves. It's more difficult to disclose the desert experiences, the hard and the dry times, the times of pain and sorrow, the times of failure and regret. It is the dark times which provide the contrasts by which the grace, mercy, and forgiveness of God are made clearer. Without the story of our desert wanderings we may be tempted to give ourselves credit rather than God. Ultimately, our journey as transitional persons is really God's story.

Third, identify your Jordan experiences, your times of renewal and restoration following a difficult journey. Most people labor under the impression that the work of God in our lives has only a starting place, a time of redemption. Subsequent times of renewal are vitally important as well.

The pace and pulse of a life in Christ must be real in order for it to be believed. The romantic version of faith doesn't wash in today's world. People want to know about the downs as well as the ups. They want to know there is help in the midst of failure as well as prevention from failure. The sentimental sheen has been worn off the stories of faith. The stories of our Jordans are what make us believable.

Finally, to complete this memorial, who are heroes and heroines of your past? Who was useful in your life? What are their names? What did they do? Maybe someone else was a transitional person in your family. You'll be encouraged when you recognize those who have contributed to your journey.

STONES IN BUILDING A MEMORIAL

We suggest you begin building your memorial with *the stone of faith.* Through whom did the gospel become a reality in your family? How and when did it happen?

What about *the stone of courage?* Stories of transitional people inevitably involve narratives of great courage and boldness. Whether large or small, these stones are necessary in the orchestration of change. Life doesn't change until someone takes "the road less traveled." Who was that traveler in your family?

And, *the stone of endurance?* Who wouldn't quit in your family? Who kept pushing ahead? What about the conditions that surrounded your journey as a transitional person? How many times did you want to stop? Why didn't you? What kept you going?

There are other stones you may wish to add: stones of love, compassion, patience, boldness, loyalty, sacrifice. Build your memorial creatively and share its specifics with your fellow travelers. Choose the stones that are important to you. It will be of significance to you to share this with someone who will want to know, "What do these stones mean?" We wish you God's grace and the power of God's Spirit as you go through your Red Sea, wander in your Sinai, or cross your Jordan. Go with faith, courage, and endurance.

Shalom.
DENNIS AND LUCY GUERNSEY

Appendix

FAMILY HISTORY QUESTIONNAIRE

1. Please list the names of all members of your immediate family (husband, wife, children and their families). Please include date of birth and occupation for each individual, along with date of death and cause of death for any deceased members (attach additional sheet if necessary).

Name	*B-day*	*Occupation*	*Date/cause of death*
			(if applicable)

2. Please list dates of marriage for all applicable family members. Include any previous marriages, as well as current ones. List dates for any separations or divorces.

3. Please list the education level of each family member. Include the names of any post-high school institutions attended.

4. Please briefly characterize the ethnic background of your family.

5. Please briefly characterize the religious background of your family.

6. Please list dates (and location) of any major family moves. Include a brief statement of the reason for the move.

7. Please list names and occupations of any other people who have lived with your family, or anyone whom you would say has had a significant influence on your family (if the latter, blease briefly characterize the influence).

8. Please describe your relations with your extended family.

9. For all family members (include extended family to the extent that you have that knowledge), please indicate any of the following (briefly describe the problem, and include date or dates of occurrence):
    Serious medical, behavioral, or emotional problems:

    Job problems:

    Drug or alcohol problems:

    Serious problems with the law:

10. For all family members (include relations among extended family members, not just among your own family or between a member of your immediate family and an extended family member), indicate and briefly characterize any relationships that are (were):

Especially close:

Distant or conflictual:

Cut off from each other:

Overly dependent upon each other:

11. Please list here all family members mentioned in this questionnaire with a brief statement that describes them and / or their role in the family.

Thank you for your time. Please include any comments you have or any other information about your family that you feel is relevant but not covered in this questionnaire.